# LITERATURE FROM CRESCENT MOON PUBLISHING

*Sexing Hardy: Thomas Hardy and Feminism*
by Margaret Elvy

*Thomas Hardy's Jude the Obscure: A Critical Study*
by Margaret Elvy

*Thomas Hardy's Tess of the d'Urbervilles: A Critical Study*
by Margaret Elvy

*Stepping Forward: Essays, Lectures and Interviews*
by Wolfgang Iser

*Andrea Dworkin*
by Jeremy Mark Robinson

*German Romantic Poetry: Goethe, Novalis, Heine, Hölderlin*
by Carol Appleby

*Cavafy: Anatomy of a Soul*
by Matt Crispin

*Rilke: Space, Essence and Angels in the Poetry of Rainer Maria Rilke*
by B.D. Barnacle

*Rimbaud: Arthur Rimbaud and the Magic of Poetry*
by Jeremy Mark Robinson

*Shakespeare: Love, Poetry and Magic in Shakespeare's Sonnets and Plays*
by B.D. Barnacle

*Feminism and Shakespeare*
by B.D. Barnacle

*The Poetry of Landscape in Thomas Hardy*
by Jeremy Mark Robinson

*D.H. Lawrence: Infinite Sensual Violence*
by M.K. Pace

*D.H. Lawrence: Symbolic Landscapes*
by Jane Foster

*The Passion of D.H. Lawrence*
by Jeremy Mark Robinson

*Samuel Beckett Goes Into the Silence*
by Jeremy Mark Robinson

*In the Dim Void: Samuel Beckett's Late Trilogy:*
*Company, Ill Seen, Ill Said and Worstward Ho*
by Gregory Johns

*Andre Gide: Fiction and Fervour in the Novels*
by Jeremy Mark Robinson

*The Ecstasies of John Cowper Powys*
by A.P. Seabright

*Amorous Life: John Cowper Powys and the Manifestation of Affectivity*
by H.W. Fawkner

*Postmodern Powys: New Essays on John Cowper Powys*
by Joe Boulter

*Rethinking Powys: Critical Essays on John Cowper Powys*
edited by Jeremy Mark Robinson

*Thomas Hardy and John Cowper Powys: Wessex Revisited*
by Jeremy Mark Robinson

*Thomas Hardy: The Tragic Novels*
by Tom Spenser

*Julia Kristeva: Art, Love, Melancholy, Philosophy, Semiotics*
by Kelly Ives

*Luce Irigaray: Lips, Kissing, and the Politics of Sexual Difference*
by Kelly Ives

*Helene Cixous I Love You: The Jouissance of Writing*
by Kelly Ives

Emily Dickinson: *Selected Poems*
selected and introduced by Miriam Chalk

*Petrarch, Dante and the Troubadours: The Religion of Love and Poetry*
by Cassidy Hughes

Dante: *Selections From the Vita Nuova*
translated by Thomas Okey

Friedrich Hölderlin: *Selected Poems*
translated by Michael Hamburger

Rainer Maria Rilke: *Selected Poems*
translated by Michael Hamburger

*Walking In Cornwall*
by Ursula Le Guin

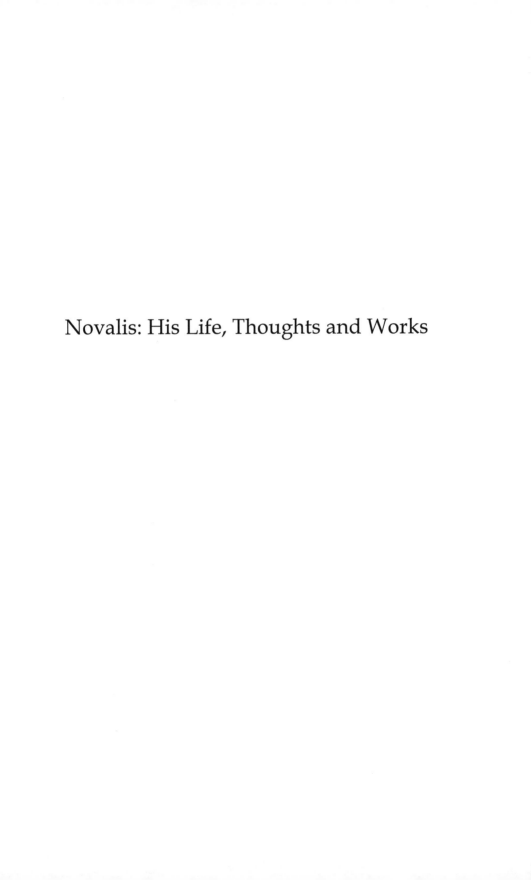

Novalis: His Life, Thoughts and Works

# Novalis: His Life, Thoughts and Works

## NOVALIS

Translated and Edited by M.J. Hope
Edited by Carol Appleby

CRESCENT MOON

CRESCENT MOON PUBLISHING
P.O. Box 1312, Maidstone
Kent, ME14 5XU
Great Britain
www.crmoon.com

First published 1891. This edition 2018.
© Carol Appleby 2018.

Printed and bound in the U.S.A.
Set in Book Antiqua 10 on 14pt.
Designed by Radiance Graphics.

British Library Cataloguing in Publication data available

ISBN-13 9781861715760 (Pbk)
ISBN-13 9781861717160 (Hbk)

# CONTENTS

A NOTE ON THE TEXT

The text is from *Novalis: His Life, Thoughts and Works*, edited and translated by M.J. Hope, published by A.C. McClurg, Chicago, 1891.

Novalis

# TRANSLATOR'S PREFACE

## By M.J. Hope

'Few authors have ever produced so great an impression on the world of German thought as Novalis' wrote Tieck in 1846. That the impression was no ephemeral one was proved in 1872, when a monument was erected to his memory at Weissenfels by his admiring countrymen.

Since his death the many practical discoveries which he foretold have almost revolutionized life in its material aspect, but the realm of conjecture in which his keen intellect revelled remains as ever a world of mystery.

The absorbing whirl of life leaves less and less time for abstract thought; the clamorous duties of the present shut out the unseen; men content themselves with the worn-out thoughts of others, passed on from one generation to another, like time-worn coins. Provided the coin will pass, it matters not to them if the image is obliterated and the intrinsic value apocryphal.

Thinkers such as Pascal, Coleridge, and Novalis, arise at intervals to rouse men's minds from their lazy acquiescence in the conventional.

All who are not bound by the chains of dogma or prejudice, all who are real seekers after truth, must, as Tieck says, receive with gratitude these sparks and flashes of a deep-thinking spirit.

The truly religious, the philosopher, and the metaphysician will be stirred in the depth of their beings by the keen remarks which disclose so many hidden treasures. These must not be read merely for amusement, but studied with the same attention required for those masterpieces of art and immutable mysteries of nature which kindle new life in the soul.

In this age, when the hereditary evolution of character has attracted so much attention, it is curious to cast a glance on the people and circumstances which, consciously or unconsciously, moulded our philosopher's life.

Ulrich Erasmus von Hardenberg, his father, was a man of strong passionate character, honest, upright, and intensely active. He was born in 1738, and though trained at Göttingen, he forsook his practical work in the "Salines" to go through the Seven Years' War in the Hanoverian legion. After the peace he established himself at Wiederstedt, a picturesque old mansion – formerly a convent – on the spurs of the Hartz, which had been a hundred years in the family.

The smallpox was then the scourge of Europe. It broke out in the village near his home with such severity that not a household escaped from its cruel ravages. Much alarmed for the safety of his young wife, Hardenberg hurried her to Graitz, to the house of her relation, Count Reuss. All in vain, the dreaded disease appeared, and in a few days ended her life.

Hardenberg was crushed by the heavy blow; but instead of idly giving way to his grief, he hurried back to the village of Wiederstedt, sent for a doctor and medicines, and personally nursed the sick and buried the dead.

Looking on his wife's death as a punishment for his past life, he threw himself with all the ardour of his nature into the views of Doddridge and Wesley. Later on in his life, the influence of Zinzendorf and the Hermhüter community softened the harshness of some of his convictions.

A year after his wife's death he married a young cousin whom his mother had taken under her protection.

The first time Freiherr von Hardenberg met her, he asked her her name.

"Bernardine," she replied.

"What an absurd name! Have you no other?"

"Augusta."

"Well, then, I shall call you so henceforth."

Bemardine von Bölzig did not conceal her annoyance at such peremptory treatment; but, in spite of it, a few weeks convinced her of her cousin's noble and generous character, and they were married 1st July, 1770.

Although it turned out in many respects a happy marriage, it was unfortunate for the children that while Augusta was yielding to a fault with her husband, she so dreaded the vehemence of his character and the severity of his principles, that she always strove to hide the children's faults from him, and thus paved the way for much future misunderstanding.

Soon the old home at Wiederstedt resounded with the merry voices of a troop of children, who played fantastic games in the ancient, gloomy hall, woke the echoes in the long corridors where nuns had formerly trod with noiseless step, and chased one another up and down the narrow winding stairs, faintly lighted by the slits in the thick walls, or made the roomy old barn, formerly the convent chapel, the scene of their weird acting, as the spirits of fire, air, earth, and water.

The children were thrown entirely on their own resources for amusement, as their father avoided all intercourse even with his neighbours, deeming it dangerous and unchristian. At first Augusta strove to overcome this strong prejudice, as she foresaw the dangers of this complete isolation for her children; but in this matter, as in all else, the strong will of Hardenberg carried the day.

The more restricted the circle in which young people grow up, the stronger are the impressions produced on them by those with whom they come in contact; and there can be little doubt that the weird and fantastic element in Novalis received a great stimulus from his boyish rambles among the picturesque scenery of the Wipperthale, and his intercourse with the grave, laborious peasants of that region, who were mostly miners.

Two frequent visitors opened up for him a vista into the unknown world of men and action.

The one was his mother's brother, Captain von Bölzig, who had been all through the Seven Years' War, and who never wearied in telling his eager listeners the story of his campaigns and battles. He was an enthusiastic admirer of Frederick the Great, and had zealously adopted his views as to absolute freedom in religious matters, urging on his strict brother-in-law the fact that there was more uprightness and fear of God in Frederick's army than had ever been attained by the "Wöllner'schen Edicts."

The other was his father's elder brother, a man of wealth and position, Landcomthur of Lucklum, in Brunswick,[1] who intervened on behalf of his favourite nephew when he fell into disgrace with his father for challenging the narrow and illogical views of the pastor chosen to instruct him in the tenets of the Moravians.

Suddenly transplanted into the luxurious and intellectual home of the Landcomthur, Novalis threw himself with ardour on the treasures which a large and well-chosen library offered him, and his thoughts were enlarged and animated by the intercourse with the numerous guests, whom the Landcomthur's hospitality gathered around him.

A year at the Gymnasium at Eisleben, with a genial master and industrious fellow-students, did much to prepare Novalis for the higher studies at Jena, where he was sent in 1791 to study law.

Jena took at that time the highest rank among the German universities. The professors, Griesbach, Reinhold (who had been a Jesuit) and Schiller, opened up a world of intellectual attraction to the ardent young student. Schiller won his warmest admiration, and he spoke of him as "the most perfect type of humanity since the days of the Greeks."

---

1 Landcomthur or Commander of Knights of the Teutonic order, a much higher dignity than Knight-Commander.

Not even the ardour with which he threw himself into his studies, nor the fascination such congenial society exercised over him, caused Novalis to neglect the mother to whom he was so devoted. He wrote to her in the summer of 1791: –

"I know how pleased you are when I write to you, though I need no such spur to arouse my remembrance of you. Your image is ever with me; and I conjure up the happy scenes of the past so associated with you, and the future, which will ever be animated by your influence urging me on to attempts which by myself I dare not venture on. To whom do all men who have ever striven to work for mankind owe their zeal? To their mothers. You did more to develop my mind than anyone, and all that I may ever accomplish is your doing, and will prove my gratitude to you. Are you really stronger? I trust you are as well as I hope you are, and that we may all look forward to a long series of years, the happiness of which is centred in you."

His mother had for many years been too ill to take any active part in the household; this had added to the gloom of his home, banishing all fun and frolic, and creating a permanent home atmosphere of anxiety. This was not displeasing to the head of the household, who looked askant on all social intercourse. Even when the mother recovered health and strength, no change was made in a life which had grown habitual, and which suited the simple tastes and austere principles of Caroline, the eldest daughter. The sons, as they grew up, were sociable, gay, and lively, but had to conceal these tendencies from their father, who looked upon all amusement as a crime.

At Leipzig Novalis and his brother Erasmus threw themselves with the eagerness of youth into social pleasures, and were received in the best society. The most flattering opinions were expressed as to their talents and personal charms. Devoted to one another as the brothers were, it was a terrible grief when the increasing delicacy of Erasmus ended this happy period.

Novalis had drawn down on himself the displeasure of his uncle by neglecting the study of law for the more congenial pursuits of philosophy, chemistry, and mathematics. The Landcomthur, knowing his nephew's talents, was keen to launch him in public life, and looked down on abstract studies. At the same time, his father was much irritated because Novalis, being disappointed in love, entreated permission to become a soldier. "I need discipline" – he wrote to his father –

> and shall have to educate myself all my life. A character such as mine needs contact with actuality. A narrow circle stifles me. I require the incitements of duty to my fatherland; I must learn to bear blame, and be led by honour. The subordination, order, and monotony of a soldier's life will be very helpful to me. My romantic tendency will be corrected by the practical, unromantic duties of my life. As to annoyances, I can live them down. I should be no son of yours if any fear of death held me back. I have an indifference to life which will seem to you paradoxical. I am convinced that many other losses are far more grievous. Life is not a goal, only a means; and when one passes from this planet one leaves behind little which one can regret."

Neither father nor uncle found these reasons at all convincing, nor gave the least encouragement to Novalis to throw away the fruits of his studies. It was deemed better for him to leave Leipzig and enter the University of Wittenberg in 1793.

Here Novalis worked hard, but he was in what Goethe has aptly named the "Sturm und Drang" period of existence. He was a charming companion, and this led him into expenses for which he was severely blamed by both uncle and father.

To a severe letter, intimating that they had lost all confidence in him, Novalis answered most characteristically. In the commencement he acknowledged his extravagance, and assured them that they need apprehend no such fault for the future; but that he could not understand why, when they knew so well his character and his devotion to the work which he hoped would one day make him independent, they should stigmatize him as a hypocrite and irreclaimable character on account of a venial fault.

To all these causes of misunderstanding was added another, arising from the exciting news from France. The seniors of the family were filled with horror and wrath. "The French are mad!"

exclaimed Novalis' father; and throwing down the newspaper containing the trial of Louis XVI, he vowed never to touch one again – a vow which he kept till his dying day to the letter, although he had no objection to receive information at second-hand on the events of the day.

The young men were, on their side, captivated by the revolutionary principles. Looking around on the effete, crumbling little principalities which encumbered Germany, diffusing nought but formalism and corruption, stifling all free thought and paralysing action, they felt intense sympathy with a movement which broke down mouldering barriers between caste and caste, and snapped the time-worn bands of custom and usage. The air of freedom intoxicated the ardent souls of the imaginative and unpractical, and they believed that a new and glorious era was at hand.

This was at the root of all the differences between such a loving father as Hardenberg and his son. The struggle of the epoch was reflected in their lives; they each misunderstood the other, nor did they find the key to unlock the riddle on this side of the grave. The political divergence of ideas was so keen, that the Freiherr saw all his son's doings in a distorted light, and mourned over him as a hopeless unbeliever while he was writing hymns which stirred the heart of Germany. After his son's death, he heard one of these for the first time at his own Moravian church, and was so moved by it, that hurrying to the pastor at the conclusion of the service, he inquired who was its author.

"Your son," was the reply, an answer which was a revelation to the kind-hearted but prejudiced man, who had refused to acknowledge old truths when presented in a new form.

Now, as then, evolution is ever at work. The outer forms of truth vary with the feeling and knowledge of the epoch; but a clear, searching gaze recognizes the old truth and the old lie under whatever disguise they may appear. Happy are those who are not baffled by appearances, but who can discern the underlying power amid the forest of words. The Freiherr,

* 19

measuring all surrounding events by his own standard, saw in all the political changes a menace to Christianity, and therefore opposed all his son's opinions with vehemence; while the Landcomthur, his brother, resisted angrily all encroachments on the old-established aristocratic basis of society, and looked down with ill-concealed contempt on his cousin the State Chancellor's new title of Graf (Prince), which he called "an imposition on posterity."

A letter to his dearly-loved brother, Erasmus, at this time gives a curious insight into Novalis' feelings: –

> "As to your quarrels with those two old-fashioned heads I will only say one thing, that in such a controversy there is the double danger of being one-sided and obstinate, and of doing injustice to one's opponent. That everything has two sides is a thrashed-out commonplace, which life makes only too clear. The true ingredients of a genuinely philosophic life are found only by silent reflection on the innumerable influences which affect our fellow creatures, and by boundless consideration for them, and a toleration which can scarcely be carried too far."

About this time Novalis was offered by his cousin, the Minister von Hardenberg, an official appointment at Berlin. His father was already irritated at his cousin for accepting the title of Graf, and refused to let his son have any connection with one so worldly, though his own pride peeped out amusingly in his wrathful comment on the proposal that he should apply for a patent of nobility for himself and his sons. He wrote contemptuously to the Landcomthur,

> "A poor count is an absurdity, I cannot leave a fortune to my children, and I much prefer an old Freiherr to a newly-baked Graf."

Novalis was keenly anxious to accept, but yielded to his father's persuasions that he should temporarily occupy himself by learning practical business from the Kreis Amtmann Just, until matters were settled.

An entirely altered view of life took rise from this change of scene, as Novalis fell deeply in love with Sophie von Kühn, and no longer wished to enter upon an official existence. Never was anything more idyllic than this love affair. Sophie was but fourteen, a gay, beautiful child, unlike anyone Novalis had ever met; while her merry, cheerful home formed an absolute contrast to the gloom and restraint of Wiessenfels, where his parents were now living.

Sophie became his ideal, the dream of his life; his enthusiastic devotion was like that of Dante to Beatrice. Every spare moment was now spent at her home at Grüningen, and her still young and winning mother received Novalis and all his brothers as welcome guests.

At first Erasmus, his favourite brother, threw cold water on the idyll. Sophie was young, she knew nothing of the world, she was beautiful, she might change, she might be spoiled by attentions, and so on; Novalis had been ridiculously hasty. What? Fall in love; make up his mind for life on the strength of a quarter of an hour's talk with a lovely fascinating girl? It was ridiculous.

On nearer acquaintance, Erasmus became as charmed with Grüningen as his elder brother, and one of his letters contains a delightful sketch of Grüningen and its inhabitants. The jolly, rollicking master of the house (Sophie's step-father), Herr von Roggenthin, always busy and full of jokes; the mother, with her angel's face and deep blue eyes (second in beauty only to Sophie's), so full of love and sympathy for everyone; Sophie, herself, an ideal of grace and beauty; the funny little Fritz, and the angel child Mimi; good Danscour, the French governess, ever ready to defend Novalis' interests against possible rivals who came wooing, attracted by the fame of Sophie's good looks and housewifely ways.

The summer of 1795 fled rapidly and happily past in spite of the uncertainty which Novalis felt respecting his father's concurrence in his choice. He was hard at work with Just, and, in spite of his love affair, carried on a correspondence with his brothers on all the abstract points which absorbed his active mind.

Autumn brought a cruel blow in Sophie's severe illness, and home-life was rendered even harder than usual by the presence of the Landcomthur, who violently opposed all idea of Novalis' marriage, and stirred up the Freiherr against it also, proving, with the hard logic of common sense, that a poor girl threatened with delicate health would be a lifelong hindrance to his nephew's career.

Trembling for Sophie's life, Novalis describes himself as like a gambler whose whole existence is bound up in one stake – whether a blossom should belong to this world or the next?

"I could not have endured my many anxieties and annoyances, could not have slept, worked, thought, and spoken like other men, had I not buried myself in the pursuit of knowledge, striving to forget the dreamworld of fate"

thus he wrote to Sophie's aunt.

"There alone bloom the hopes which vanish here from my sight, all that keeps me back as regards this life are steps onward in my thought-life, the sword which cuts keenest to the heart turns into a magic staff, the ashes of the earthly rose give birth to the heavenly. As my hopes die out, my fancy grows; and when nought remains to me but a stone, fancy will raise me above it, and restore to me what I have lost."

Sophie's death on the 19th of March, 1797, was a cruel blow. For three years she had never been out of his thoughts; for her sake he worked, for her he had reconciled himself to a life of prosaic routine – the very opposite of his youthful dreams and ambition. For a time he was overwhelmed, so much so that he failed to realize the critical condition of his faithful Erasmus, who returned home but to die of decline.

Terrible was the struggle of his mind, but at last peace, heavenly peace, conquered the storm of despair, and Novalis emerged from the heavy cloud of sorrow a Christian and a poet.

Again the conventional barrier of words caused fresh misunderstanding between him and the Freiherr. The phraseology of

Wesley and the Moravians jarred on the sensitive nature of the poet philosopher; he meant what they meant, but expressed the fresh thoughts of a cultivated mind in a freer and more philosophic phraseology. Novalis could only express his deepest feeling in song free from all stamp of sectarianism. The Freiherr recoiled from individuality in religion as blasphemy, and only long years after his son's death looked at his writings and acknowledged that, in spite of much he disagreed with, they strengthened his hopes of a future meeting.

From this time, however, there was an entire relaxation in the strict home rules. Novalis was free to come and go as he liked, stay with his friends or receive them at Weissenfels as he chose.

The few remaining years of his life were devoted to practical work, acquiring knowledge, and chronicling some of his ideas and feelings. He was indifferent to renown as a writer, hence the few things which were published were signed Novalis, a name which had belonged to a branch of his family known in the sixteenth century as de Novali. These he looked on with indifference, and it needed all the persuasions of his friends to induce him to consent to their publication.

The fragments which remain, and the two unfinished romances, seem like the rich collections of an artist for future use. Intellect, feeling, reflection are there; but time failed to work them up into the harmonious whole which the author aimed at. He said himself, "'Ofterdingen' is too hard and crude; the middle tints are wanting, and my work is incomplete and fragmentary, the best form for what is unfinished."

His favourite production was *Hymns to the Night*, but to the world at large his *Hymns* spoke as none had done since the days of Luther. They were free from all sectarian bias, suitable for all Christian churches, and recall by their simplicity and poetry the earliest hymns of the Church. Tieck, Schlegel, and Schiller, thought highly of the young genius, and mourned over his untimely death. Tieck, by his carelessness in editing his works, gave to the world an impression that Novalis had Roman Catholic tendencies. He massed all his poetry together as the natural expression of his own feelings, not perceiving that the hymns to the Virgin were merely intended to fill a niche in the *Ofterdingen* romance, where they express the sentiments of the Middle Ages.

This gave rise to the impression that Novalis died a Roman Catholic; and the confusion seems to have even pained men like Just,[2] who knew him best.

Once more his path was brightened by love, and his life soothed by the sympathy of a congenial heart. In 1798 he made up his mind to marry Julie Charpentier, a very accomplished and lovely girl, whom he frequently met in the course of his life at Freiberg. The engagement was known to all the family, but only officially announced to the old Freiherr in 1800. As usual, objections were raised; but matters were smoothed over when Novalis received an independent appointment. He was at the very goal of his hopes when he was seized with a sudden attack of haemorrhage on hearing of an accident which had happened to a favourite little brother. His health, which had for long been in a critical state, utterly failed, and after passing a short time in painless prostration, still occupied with his favourite studies, and, in the enjoyment of Julie's society, he softly fell asleep to the sound of music.

The last entries in his diary clearly reveal his thoughts at that time.

"What is an anxious hour, a painful night, a sad month, in comparison with an eternity of happiness?"

"All that we call chance is ordered by God. Did not Christ Himself see the inexpressible grief of His mother? He knows what we feel when our sorrows react on those we love."

"When one realizes that the world is God's kingdom, when that idea permeates our whole being, we pass amid the gloom and sorrow of this earthly life full of peace and heavenly composure."

---

2 Just wrote the short life of Novalis, which follows the Preface.

"Despair comes from the devil; courage and hope from God."

"Bodily restlessness would be endurable if only it did not affect the mind. One cannot control the body, but one must seek to obtain mastery on the mind."

"Once the soul is at peace the body will rest too."

"The terrible evil of falsehood is that it surrounds us with a false world."

"Courage strengthens. God's will be done – not mine. Patience and resignation are the best helpmates. There is nought more difficult than to have patience with oneself, to bear one's own weakness."[3]

No more able critic has ever treated of Novalis than Carlyle, and a few extracts from his "Essay On Novalis" will do more to enable the general reader to comprehend the scope and value of these collected fragments than either praise or blame from a less competent author.

"We reckon it more profitable, in almost any case, to have to do with men of depth than with men of shallowness: and were it possible, we would read no book that was not written by one of the former class. Such of our readers as at all participate in this predilection will not blame us for bringing them acquainted with Novalis, a man of the most indisputable talent, poetical and philosophical; whose opinions, extraordinary, nay altogether wild and baseless as they often appear, are not without a strict coherence in his own mind, and will lead any other mind, that examines them faithfully, into endless considerations; opening the strangest enquiries, new truths, or new possibilities of truth, a whole unexpected world of thought, where, whether for belief or denial, the deepest questions await us.

"His writings come before us with every disadvantage; they are the posthumous works of a man cut off in early life, while his opinions, far from being matured for the public eye, were still lying crude and disjointed before his own; for the most part written in the shape of detached aphorisms, none of them, as he himself says, 'untrue or unimportant to his own mind,' but requiring to be remodelled, expanded, compressed, as the matter cleared up more and more into logical unity; at best but fragments of a great scheme which he did not

3 Friedrich von Hardenberg (genannt Novalis.) Eine Nach lese aus der Quellen des Banülienarchivs herausgegeben von lenem Mitglied der Familie. – Gotha: F.A. Perthes, 1873.

live to realize.

"If his editors, Friederich Schlegel and Ludwig Tieck, declined commenting on these writings, we may well be excused for declining to do so. 'It cannot be our purpose here', says Tieck, 'to recommend the following works or to judge them; probable as it must be that any judgment delivered at this stage would be premature: for a spirit of such originality must first be comprehended, his will understood, and his loving intention felt and replied to; so that not till his ideas have taken root in other minds, and brought forth new ideas, shall we see rightly, from the historical sequence, what place he himself occupied, and what relation to his country he actually bore.'

"Meanwhile Novalis is a figure of such importance in German literature that no student can pass him by. Experience, the grand schoolmaster, seems to have taught Novalis the great doctrine of Renunciation very early, by the wreck of his first passionate wish; and herein lies the real influence of Sophie on his character; an influence which, as we imagine, many other things might and would have equally exerted: for it is less the severity of the Teacher than the aptness of the Pupil that secures the lesson; nor do the purifying effects of frustrated hope and affection, which in this world will ever be homeless, depend on the worth or loveliness of its objects, but on that of the heart which cherished it, and can draw mild wisdom from so severe a disappointment. We do not say that Novalis continued the same as if this young maiden had not been; causes and effects connecting every man and thing with every other extend through all time and space; but surely it appears unjust to represent him as so altogether pliant in the hands of accident, a mere pipe for Fortune to play tunes on; and which sounded a mystic, deep, almost unearthly melody, simply because a young woman was beautiful and mortal.

"The slightest perusal of his writings indicates to us a mind of wonderful depth and originality; but, at the same time, of a nature or habit so abstruse, and altogether different from anything we ourselves have experience of, that to penetrate fairly into its essential character, much more to picture it forth in visual distinctness, would be an extremely difficult task; for Novalis belongs to that class of persons who do not recognize the 'syllogistic method' as the chief organ for investigating truth, or feel themselves bound at all times to stop short where its light fails them. Many of his opinions he would despair of proving in the most patient court of law, and would remain well content that they should be disbelieved there. He much loved, and had assiduously studied, Jacob Boehme and other mystical writers; and was openly enough in good part a Mystic himself. Not what we English in common speech call a Mystic, which means only a man whom we do not understand, and in self-defence reckon, or would fain reckon, a dunce. Novalis was a Mystic, or had affinity with mysticism in the primary and true meaning of that word, exemplified in some shape among our own Puritan Divines, and which as this day carries no opprobrium with it in Germany or, except among certain more unimportant classes, in any other country.

"Nevertheless, with all due tolerance or reverence for Novalis' mysticism, the question still returns on us: How shall we understand it, and in any measure shadow it forth? How may that spiritual condition which by its own account is like pure light, colourless, formless, infinite, be represented by mere logic painters, mere engravers we might say, who, except copper and burin, producing the most finite black-on-white, have no means of representing anything? 'What is Mysticism?' says Novalis. 'What should be mystically treated? Religion, Love, Nature, Polity. All select things have a reference to mysticism. If all men were but one pair of lovers the difference between mysticism and non-mysticism were at an end.' In which little sentence, unhappily, our reader obtains no clearness – feels rather as if looking into darkness visible. We must beg of him to keep up his spirits; perhaps some faint, far-off view of that same mysterious mysticism may rise on us. Novalis sought, as Tieck says, to open out a new path in philosophy, to unite philosophy with religion. His metaphysical creed, so far as we gather from these writings, appears synonymous with Fichte's, and may be classed under the head of Kantism, or German metaphysics generally.

"Novalis was deeply impressed with these principles. Naturally a deep, religious, contemplative spirit; purified by harsh affliction, familiar in the 'Sanctuary of Sorrow,' he comes before us as the most ideal of all Idealists. For him the material creation is but an appearance, a typical shadow in which the Deity manifests Himself to man. Not only has the unseen world a reality, but the only reality; the rest being not metaphorically, but literally, and in scientific strictness, 'a show'; in the words of the poet, 'Sound and smoke veiling the splendour of heaven.' The invisible world is near us, or, rather, it is here, in us and about us; were the fleshly coil removed the glories of the unseen were even now around us, as the ancients fabled of the spheral music.

"The aim of Novalis' philosophy is to establish the Majesty of Reason, in that stricter sense; to conquer for it all provinces of human thought, and everywhere reduce its vassal Understanding into fealty, the right and only useful relation for it. Mighty tasks in this sort lay before him, of which in these writings we trace only scattered indications. One characteristic is his way of viewing nature rather in the concrete, not analytically and as a divisible aggregate, but as a selfsubsistent universally connected whole. This also is perhaps a fruit of his idealism.

"As a poet Novalis is no less Idealistic than as a philosopher. His poems are breathings of a high, devout soul, feeling always that here he has no home, but looking as in clear vision to a city 'that hath foundations.' He loves external nature with a singular depth; nay, we might say, he reverences her, and holds unspeakable communings with her; for nature is no longer dead, hostile matter, but the veil and mysterious garment of the Unseen, as it were, the voice with which the Deity proclaims Himself to man. These two qualities – his pure religious temper, and heartfelt love of Nature – bring him into true poetic relation both with the spiritual and material world, and con-stitute his chief worth as a Poet; for which art he seems to have originally a genuine but no exclusive endowment.

"His moral persuasions, as evinced in his writings and his life, derive themselves naturally enough from the same source. It is the morality of a man to whom the earth and all its glories are in truth a vapour and a dream, and the beauty of goodness the only *real* possession. Poetry, Virtue, Religion, which for other men have but, as it were, a tradition-ary and imagined existence, are for him the everlasting basis of the universe, and all earthly acquirements; all with which Ambition, Hope, Fear can tempt us to toil and sin are in very deed but a picture of the brain, some reflex shadowed on the mirror of the Infinite, but in themselves air and nothingless. Thus to live in that light of reason, to have even while here, and encircled with the Vision of Existence, our abode in that Eternal City, is the highest and sole duty of man.

"For one thing, either Novalis, with Tieck and Schlegel at his back, are men in a state of derangement, or there is more in heaven and earth than has been dreamt of in our philosophy.

"Novalis nowhere specially records his creed. He many times expresses or implies a zealous, heartfelt belief in the Christian system, yet with such adjuncts and co-existing persuasions as to us might seem rather surprising.

"For the great body of readers we are aware there can be little profit in Novalis, who rather employs our time than helps to kill it. To others, who prize truth as the end of all reading – especially to that class who cultivate moral science as the development of purest and highest truth – we can recommend the perusal and reperusal of Novalis with perfect confidence. If they feel with us that the most profitable employment any book can give them is to study honestly some earnest, deep-minded, truth-loving man, to work their way into his manner of thought till they see the world with his eyes, feel as he felt, and judge as he judged, neither believing nor denying till they can in some measure so feel and judge, then we may assert *that few books known to us are more worthy of attention than this.*

"They will find it an unfathomed mine of philosophical ideas, where the keenest intellect may have occupation enough; and in such occupat-ion, without looking farther, reward enough. All this if the reader proceed on candid principles; if not, it will be all otherwise. To no man so much as Novalis is that famous motto applicable –

✴ 28

"'Leser, wie gefall'ich Dir?
Leser, wie gefällst Du mir?'

'Reader, how likest thou me?
Reader, how like I thee?'

"For the rest, it were a false proceeding did we attempt any formal character of Novalis in this place; did we pretend with such means as ours to reduce that extraordinary nature under common formularies, and in a few words sum up the net total of his worth and worthlessness. The kind words, 'amiable enthusiast,' 'poetic dreamer,' or the unkind ones, 'German mystic,' 'crackbrained rhapsodist,' are easily spoken and written, but would avail little in this instance. If we are not altogether mistaken, Novalis cannot be ranged under any one of these noted categories, but belongs to a higher and much less known one, the significance of which is perhaps also worth studying – at all events, will not till after long study become clear to us.

"We might say that the chief excellence we have remarked in Novalis is his wonderful subtlety of intellect; his power of intense abstraction, of pursuing the deepest and most evanescent ideas through their thousand complexities, as it were with lynx vision, and to the very limits of human thought. He was well skilled in mathematics; but his is a far finer species of endowment than any required in mathematics, where the mind, from the very beginning of Euclid to the end of Laplace, is assisted with visible symbols, with safe *implements* for thinking – nay, at least in what is called the higher mathematics, has often little more than a mechanical superintendence to exercise over these. This power of abstract meditation, when it is so sure and clear as we sometimes find it in Novalis, is a much higher and rarer one; its element is not mathematics, but that *mathesis* of which it has been truly said many a great calculist has not even a notion. In this power, truly, so far as logical and not moral power is concerned, lies the summary of all philosophic talent, which talent Novalis possessed in a very high degree – in a higher degree than almost any other modern writer we have met with.

"There is a tenderness in Novalis, a purity, a clearness almost as of a woman; but he has not – at least, not at all in the same degree – the emphasis and force of a man. Thus in his poetic delineations he is too diluted and diffuse, not so much abounding in superfluous words as in superfluous circumstances, which, indeed, is but a degree better. In his philosophical speculations we feel as if, under a different form, the same fault were now and then manifested. Here again he seems in one sense too passive. He sits, we might say, among the rich five thousandfold combinations which his mind almost of itself presents him; but perhaps he is too lax in separating the true from the doubtful – is not even at the trouble to express his truth with any laborious accuracy. However, it should always be remembered we see them under many disadvantages, not as doctrines and delineations, but as the rude draught of such."

March 2nd, 1891.

# LIFE OF NOVALIS

# By August Coelestin Just

When one says of any man "He is a genius," the accepted meaning is, that he has the peculiar quality of mind which not only enables him to acquire science or the arts with unusual facility, but has power to produce his knowledge in an original way. If the mind takes a strong bent in one direction, either towards art or science, we say, "He has a poetical or mathematical genius." But we mean a very different thing when we say, "He is a genius." We express thereby that nature has so endowed the man that in the particular art or science to which he is devoted he is not only technically perfect, but original, and has an inherent power and adaptability which enables him not only to master difficulties with ease, but to go to the very bottom of his subject, retain dearly all he has acquired, and exercise judgment and penetration in combining the results of his researches. He must have such well-balanced powers of mind that his perseverance in work is equalled by his dexterity in practice, joined to love and delight in his occupation.

These remarks occurred to me while watching the development of Friedrich von Hardenberg's richly gifted mind.

Genius is often accused of superficiality and caprice, of preferring pleasurable to graver studies, of living in theories and abhorring practical matters. But this was not the case with Hardenberg. He was determined to study everything thoroughly and deeply, and to investigate every subject of human knowledge. Joined to this, he gave diligent heed to practical life, never shirking any detail, however irksome. In addition, his heart was open to impressions of all that nature, friendship, or love can offer; and while he laboured to develop his mind, he never ignored the claims on his affections, and gauged clearly the hearts and powers of all around him.

His early death was a great loss both to science and mankind. His education had undoubtedly done much to develop his excellent powers; all the more so, because it had been many-sided, free, often changed, and heterogeneous. Born in the higher ranks, he was the son of a good, sensible, wealthy, and highly considered man, who was closely connected with men whose birth, dignities, possessions, connections, talents, and acquirements raised them above others. The advantages arising from such a position had a great influence on Hardenberg; nor did he suffer from the corresponding drawbacks. Without ignoring the difference of position of the burghers, he divided mankind merely in two classes – the cultivated and uncultivated. The only advantages which he allowed that the upper classes possessed, were hospitality, liberal views, and education: to these latter he owed much.

He was born on the 2nd May, 1772, at the family property of Wiedestedt, and for the first few years of his life gave no indications of peculiar talent. His; health was delicate, all his faculties in a dormant state, and it required all the influence of his sister, who was not a year older, to induce him to learn the ordinary rudiments. The religious element which ruled in his home had a great effect upon his childhood, though its full power was only evidenced in the last years of his life. His father led such an active, restless life, that his manifold occupations, the duties of his calling, and his geniality prevented his occupying himself with the education of his eldest son.

The work begun by the tender, loving mother, in conjunction with his little sister, was continued by tutors. Hardenberg's mind seemed suddenly roused to activity after a severe illness; when he was about nine years old, he made surprising progress in Latin, Greek, and history. Poems and fairy tales were his favourite amusement. His brothers and sisters were his only associates. His parents were devoted to the Moravian tenets, which had brought them a peace and happiness which they longed to bequeath to their children.

The eldest daughter fulfilled this wish; not so with the eldest son. They had him instructed in theology by the pastor of the small Herrnhuter colony at Neudietendorf.

As a child, his devotional and aesthetic feelings had been satisfied with these tenets; but when his mind ripened, he rebelled against the narrow barriers which repressed his individuality and intense longing for knowledge.

He found himself in a much more congenial atmosphere when sent to his uncle, the Landcomthur Hardenberg, at Luclum, in Brunswick. The Landcomthur was a man of cultivated understanding, and possessed of a fund of knowledge; he had also an excellent collection of the best and newest publications of all kinds. This, combined with the society of clever men who frequented his house, his varied experience of the world and perfect manners, together with the high tone of his mind, and the universal respect shown him, helped to cultivate and polish young Friedrich, and further his early mental development. The boy was too independent in mind to be dazzled by mere outward advantages, or to lose his keen discernment of character, while seeking to find in every one he met fresh interests for both heart and mind.

The time approached for his entrance upon a University life. He spent the previous year at Eisleben, under the guidance of the excellent Jani, who instructed him carefully in those dead languages, the neglect of which is so much regretted both at the University and in after life.

Until now he has been under the care of his parents, his uncle, and Jani; now for the first time he entered the academic world alone. In 1790 he was sent to Jena; then, with his second brother Erasmus, to Leipzig; and finally to Wittenberg, where he concluded his academical career in 1794. It was good for him to be left to his own resources, and he gained unquestionably both independence, original views, power of research, and facility of argument.

A happy combination of circumstances favoured the development of his mental powers. Kant's philosophy was then extremely in vogue, and was being carefully revised by Reinhold and Fichte. With the latter he had much intercourse, as Graf von Hardenberg helped Fichte to meet all his college expenses. Friedrich early discovered his talent, as well as that of Schelling, who used to give private lectures on philosophy to his friends.

Although so conversant with critical philosophy, still von Hardenberg loved intercourse with men who cultivated his aesthetic and poetical genius. The spirit of the times just then brought ideas of freedom and equality, man's rights, and the principles of government under discussion. He also studied law, especially at Leipzig and Wittenberg; and attained great proficiency in both chemistry and mathematics.

On leaving Wittenberg, his father sent him to Tennstedt to be trained in practical business. There we became the most intimate friends, an intimacy which lasted until his death. From that time I can record my own personal experience of him; previously I had to trust to hearsay and the accounts of others.

I was chosen to be his teacher and guide, but in reality he was my teacher; not only because I had to exert all my faculties to satisfy his keen spirit of investigation, which could never rest satisfied with any commonplace, routine views, but principally because he broke down all the chains of pedantry and narrowness which bind the ordinary business mind, and forced me to take broader views, interesting me both by his words and writings in the two ideals which his fertile intellect conjured up, and awaking in my inert mind the dormant aesthetic tastes.

Who could have expected that this young man, in his keen desire to become a perfect man of business, would shun no exertion to obtain a complete mastery of all business forms and expressions, and would show as much zeal in acquiring absolute precision as he could have done in the most congenial study?

He never rested satisfied with any half knowledge. He was never superficial, but completely thorough in his work. His excellent gifts, the complete balance of all his powers of mind, joined to his extreme facility in apprehending a subject, rendered him thus good service. He could read a new book in one-fourth the time required by a less favoured mortal; then he would lay it aside: when weeks or months afterwards the book was discussed, he was able to bring forward all the striking points, the general scope, express a clear and distinct opinion on its merits, and why and wherefore he would or would not recommend it to his friends.

This was the system on which he read, studied, worked, and formed his opinion of men. In this way he was enabled to accomplish so much in so short a life. He was acquainted with all the new writings on science and art which belonged to his time. He carefully studied all the more important ones, and made acquaintance with many of the most celebrated learned men, informing himself as to their manner of study and composition. Amongst others, I remember Jean Paul and La Fontaine.

His favourite book in 1795 was Goethe's *Wilhelm Meister* which may be traced in his *Ofterdingen*.

The three things to which he was most devoted were *logical thought* and action, *artistic* beauty, and *science*.

His devotion to logic sometimes led him astray, so that, for example, although he hated Robespierre's reign of terror, he praised it for its logic.

In the same way he delighted a pious Roman Catholic by

praising the ecclesiastical hierarchy on account of its logical *raison d'être*: as he did so, unrolling before us the whole history of the Papacy, enriching his discourse with a rich profusion of reasons and representations, the fruit of his fancy and his intellect. His love of aesthetic beauty was equally intense. Even though his mind was not in harmony with the holy doctrines of the Scriptures, its aesthetic beauty made him love and revere the *Bible*. To be sure, the same feeling might have made him love a religion which held up the Mother of God – a Madonna – as an object of worship.

Fichte had given a new meaning to the word science, which had much weight with my friend. His keenest wish was to bring back all art and science to first principles, and raise them to the dignity of true science, uniting them all in one complete whole. According to his conviction, there was a perfect harmony and union between them. With this object, he excluded no subject from his studies (and, amongst others, diligently studied Church History at Wittenberg); and though he could not thoroughly study all, yet it is a proof of his peculiar genius that he was determined to go on doing so, and to reduce his theory to practice.

With this love of science and art, it would have been difficult for him in the twenty-fourth year of his age to devote himself to a practical life, unless his aesthetic feelings, and the longing for such a happy domestic life as he had enjoyed at home, had offered him powerful inducements to do so.

During the course of a business journey he took with me, he made the acquaintance of Sophie von Kühn, a girl of thirteen years old. She possessed the judgment of a grown-up person, joined to the attraction and animation of youth, beauty, wit, and excellence. This charming creature became his Madonna; and the hopes of one day calling her his, gave him the assurance of that happy home for which he longed. This was the secret of his resigning himself to a business life. This pleased his father, who wished him to work at some practical subject. The first sphere of his activity was the Electoral Salines (salt works). Previous to entering on his new duties, he went to Langensalza for a course of instruction in chemistry from the celebrated chemist Mingleb. In ten or twelve days he had fathomed the branch relating to his future work; and Mingleb, who was a very competent judge, always spoke of his pupil with the greatest respect

He began his novitiate in 1796, under the direction of his father, Bergrath Heun, and Bergrath Senff, who formed the Board of Directors. Each of these men contributed his best efforts to the work. The Graf von Hardenberg was indefatigable, energetic, and unwearied, sacrificing his time, his heart to it; Heun, the eldest on the Board, was, as Friedrich said, a living Archive; while Senff was well known on account of his technical knowledge.

Friedrich strove to acquire all they could teach him, and at the same time, by his father's wish, paid particular attention to the minutest detail in the practical management of the Salines. He did not, however, neglect higher studies, and besides increasing his store of knowledge, he had at this lime an engrossing interest which often took him to Jena, where he met many of his particular friends, Schlegel amongst others. Sophie had fallen seriously ill, and suffered terribly from a cruel abscess, which, in spite of all the care of Doctor Stark, had formed a sinus in connection with the liver.

The poor girl, with her mother and sister, remained several months at Jena, and here the von Hardenbergs made her acquaintance, and showed her all the affection of parents. Thus love formed another tie to Jena, which had been already endeared to Friedrich by friendship and study.

Sophie returned to her father's property in Grüningen in most delicate health, and there Friedrich paid her many visits. Her illness led him to take a great interest in medicine.

His judgment told him that recovery was impossible, but his heart rebelled against so painful a separation. He was misled by the saying, "Man can accomplish what he wills"; and he thought, "His Sophie could not die."

The struggle between reason and affection was at its height when he paid her his last visit. The result ended the struggle, for Sophie died on the 19th March, 1797.

All his earthly plans seemed crushed. He, however, was not crushed. His first letter to us at Tennstedt expressed his terrible grief, but showed also how cruel fate seemed to arouse his spirit to higher thoughts and views. The first was to my wife, a friend of long standing.

"Weissenfels, 28th March, 1797.

"Your friendly words have indeed refreshed the weary one. I have indeed suffered; and it was only yesterday evening, when writing to Carolinchen, that I felt roused. Truly I have been too much absorbed in this life; and required a powerful corrective.

"I do not mourn for Sophie; God has doubtless acted with Fatherly care for her, even though He has not granted my constant prayers. Now, Sophie must know that my wish that she should be mine was only my second desire in regard to her: the first was ever for her truest development. If I mourn, it is for my own fate; I feel confused; a sudden change is hard to bear. I must forget all my past aims and hopes. I loved this world so much, and rejoiced in all its beauties, and the happy future I pictured: – it is hard to cast all this aside. But ought not this call to consider the spiritual world, the closer union with God, and all that is highest in life, compensate me? Compensate – that sounds so hard. Sophie knows what I mean. Do you think God would be angry if I prayed, 'Father, I will complain no more; I will gladly do all I have to do; I will love Thee heartily. But wilt Thou not restore us to one another? Doubtless Sophie is one of Thy darling daughters, and Thou canst not be displeased if I still live in her and long for her.' Ah! certainly He will reunite us, as He will one day restore you to your good husband,[4] and will make you happy in this world, to reward your heavenly kindness.

"Hardenberg."

The next day he wrote to me: –

"It is a bitter-sweet remark, that misfortune increases our appreciation of friendship, or appears to increase it, because it arouses a greater demonstration of it. The joy of calm possession is unobserved; but in the feeling of loss the soul realizes to the fullest extent the value of the

[4] Professor Nurnberg, of Wittenberg, who had died two years before, my wife's first husband, and a great friend of Hardenberg's.

departed happiness. My love for Sophie seems increased by her death, and my appreciation of friendship is much keener. Your kind letters have been a comfort to me. It rejoiced me to see how you appreciated the grief which Sophie's home-going has caused me. Your reminder of the unchangeable mark it will leave in my life is consoling. This did not occur to me before: until now I have lived in the presence and hope of mere earthly bliss; now I must throw myself into the future, and live in the belief of God and immortality. It will be very difficult for me to cut myself off entirely from this world, which I studied with such devotion; it will cost me many a long hour to accomplish; but I know that man has an inherent power, which, under given circumstances, can develop an unheard-of energy.

"You would be sorry for me, if you knew of the horrors of revolt through which I have passed. I do not deny that I most dread the fossilizing of my heart. By nature I was weak, but by degrees my understanding strengthened at the expense of my heart. Sophie restored my heart to its forfeited throne. How easily may this grief again enthrone the usurper, who would doubtless take vengeance on the heart! I have already suffered from its coldness; perhaps, however, the spiritual world and its power, hitherto neglected, may save me. Every day the thought of God is dearer to me. How enchanted anyone would be who had never heard of God, if, when sorrow and misfortune overwhelmed him, the fact of a loving Father were suddenly revealed to him!

"I hope it may be so with me. Love made me interested in all human affairs. Now that is all over, cold duty must take the place of love. My business will be mere official work. Everywhere there is too much noise and bustle for me. I shall shrink into myself more and more. Thus the path to the grave will gradually become more familiar. The chasm which separates us will grow narrower day by day. Science will acquire a greater attraction for me, for I shall study with higher aims and objects.

"I will devote myself to thoughts of the unseen world and until my death, which cannot be far off, I will seek comfort with a few friends and in devotion to my duties.

"My people show me deep and silent sympathy, especially Karl and my father. The latter actually wept – the first time for many years. This loss has made this world strange to him also. Erasmus has been here for the last three weeks; he is seriously ill. My indifference to everything has prevented my suffering on his account."

Erasmus, with whom he had shared his education, his heart, and his intellect, had come home from a College of Forestry, dangerously ill – every day his death was expected.

This induced the sorrowing parents, who were deeply anxious about their eldest son, to send him to live quietly with us for some time at Tennstedt. His heart was deeply wounded, but his fancy was alert, not wildly, but under the strong restraint of judgment. At first he was unable to visit the spot where Sophie was buried, but on Easter Eve he felt able to go. He spent Easter Sunday on that hallowed spot, perhaps in accordance with the Resurrection Festival of the Brüdergemeinde. He returned in the evening calm and even cheerful. That very day he received the news of his brother's death. He uttered no complaints and shed no tears, though he spoke of him with feeling. He was so self-possessed that he even discoursed on other subjects with interest. The spiritual life of his betrothed, and his speedy reunion with her, had become the ruling thoughts of his mind. This was evidenced by the beautiful words he wrote to his third brother, Karl: "Be comforted! Erasmus has overcome. The blossoms of the dearly loved garland are being separated here, to bloom together in eternity."

His fancy flattered him with the hope that he should join his loved ones within the year. He devoted himself to Lavater's writings. For many hours every day he wrote on nature, philosophy, and eternity. He was now glad to surround himself with relics which reminded him of Sophie.

Cheerfulness gradually returned to him: he interested himself in nature, household matters, and even surprised his friends by a joking epistle about the purchase of a garden.

After a few weeks he returned to Weissenfels, devoting himself to cheer his mother and sister, after their deep distress, by taking them excursions and short journeys.

I give an extract from a letter describing one of these excursions with Landvoight, his younger brother's tutor.

"Weissenfels, 1st July, 1797.
"I have just returned from a delightful trip with the boys' tutor to the

Rosstrappe. The weather was glorious, and nothing disturbed the pleasure of the pilgrimage except weary legs. We stayed all night at Bällenstadt. We had the most lovely view from the windows of the palatial hotel: on the left, the heights beyond Quedlinburg, and the natural ruins of the so-called Devils Wall; to the right, wooded heights. The road from Bällenstadt is splendid, and offers most varied views. We passed Regenstein, a strong castle ruined in the Seven Years' War. On a spur of the Harz stands the Castle of Blankenberg; and high above among the woods, shine the roofs of Hüttenrode; beyond rise the lofty peaks of the Harz, shrouded in mantles of blue mist, like giants. The entrance of the Rosstrappe seems like the gate through which the giants may enter the valley. Destruction and loneliness herald an abode of terror. Even at Thale, where the Bude issues from the mountains among the red-roofed villages, the scattered fragments of massy rock which litter its bed announce the chaos which is at hand.

"In front of the inn stood a large waggon full of sausages" –

Here follows a very comical description of the people they met there, and the original gossiping guide, a cobbler, whom they engaged to show them the way, of whom he writes: –

"He had had many adventures among the Prussian soldiers, had gone through the Seven Years' War, and was full of experience, knowledge of the world, and courage. He complained of the invasion of his office by idle tramps, who undertook to show travellers over the Rosstrappe. There was even a cabal against him in the inn. The maid had an idiotic, stupid brother, whom she induced the host to summon whenever travellers came who were likely to give a good tip, while he was only sent for in cases of necessity. He knew, he said, that it was the usual fate of genius, and he could bear it with resignation; he was only sorry for the travellers, who went away with their curiosity unsatisfied, grumbling because the Rosstrappe had not come up to their expectations. His experience enabled him to reply to all our questions. In addition, he showed his knowledge by guessing that we came from Weissenfels by our dialect: he could not be mistaken in any German accent, he knew them all. The ascent was thus pleasantly beguiled. Once at the top, all our fatigues were amply repaid. One looks down precipices on either side, down, down into fearful chasms. The Bude can scarcely be discerned far below, amid the jagged rocks; and the rush of its waters can scarcely be heard. The rocks are grouped in quaint masses; on one side woods and precipices, on the other a glorious prospect over the plain towards Quedlinburg. The cliff by which one leaves the pass stretches right across the valley, crowned with wood; a fearful chasm separates it from the right side of the valley. A rock about a yard in length, which protrudes from the side of the precipice, is the *non plus ultra* to the curious visitor. It requires more than ordinary courage to step on to this stone and look down into the so-called 'Crown Hole.' This Crown Hole is a deep pool, in which an invaluable diadem is said to be lying, where it was dropped by the Princess whose adventure gave the name of the Rosstrappe[5] to this wild region.

"This heroic maiden was dancing with her companions on the opposite side of the chasm, still called the Dancing-hall, when surprised by a fierce and unwelcome lover, a Wendisch prince. Just in time she jumped on her favourite horse, who, with a mighty bound, crossed the yawning chasm, and deposited the brave maiden in safety at the foot of the Brocken. The traces of the horse's hoofs were pointed out by our guide; but intercourse with the world seemed to have developed his critical instinct, for even on the scene immortalized by this historic deed, he spoke of it with an incredulous sneer. It is true, however, that in such exalted regions one feels more disposed to belief than in the monotonous plains, for the surroundings were truly wonderful. Among the trees rise strange rocks, bearing the appearance of towers, gates, and lofty pillars. At last he led us out to a spot which proved his comprehension of his trade. There, in a lonely wooded wilderness, rose the towering Brocken and its companions. The guide was not a little proud of his monopoly of this view. 'None of those pretenders know it,' he asserted, with conscious pride; once he had put one to utter shame, as he was telling some visitors the Brocken could not be seen from the Rosstrappe, and even betted that no one could see it. Our guide then triumphantly led the visitors to the spot which commanded so fine a view. He told us also two gruesome tales about three children of the valley beneath, who, clambering up to fetch sticks in the forest, lost their footing, and fell over the precipice: the girl's neck was broken, one boy escaped with broken arms and legs, while the third was only slightly bruised; – also of a young hunter who ascended the Rabenstein to take an eagle's eyrie, and, once up, could not get down again. During three days all the villagers streamed up to the Rosstrappe, but no one could reach the perilous spot, or find any way to deliver the poor lad. On the last day his father, the forester stood leaning against a tree, with his rifle in his hand, looking at him wistfully. At last a bold raftsman succeeded in reaching him, and brought him safely down a rope-ladder. Afterwards, the father said that he was waiting till all attempts failed, and then he intended to shoot the lad, to save him from the pangs of death by starvation.

"We returned to the valley by an easy path."

---

5 *Rosstrappe* – a horse's hoof-mark.

He concludes with a merry and satirical account of the party assembled in the inn.

The summer passed away in visits home, little journeys, and work at the Salines. His mind recovered tone, and his health improved. He still cherished hopes of a speedy reunion with his beloved, though he no longer anticipated it as close at hand. His interest in life revived, and he reverted into the same state which he had been in before he met Sophie.

He now wished either to devote himself to the study of medicine or mining. He was more inclined to the first, but duty dictated the other.

He was already acquainted with all the latest discoveries in medicine, and wished to work out a system founded on a fixed principle of certainty.

The wishes of his father, and love for his family, towards whom he owed the duty of an eldest brother, led him to go to Freiberg, and prepare himself for further work at the Electoral Salines. This was in 1797. He now devoted himself to physics, chemistry, higher mathematics, geology, metallurgy, all of which were taught at the Mining College. His principal guide was Werner. Thus passed the year which he believed was to end his life. He still lived, and his enthusiastic love of Sophie led him again to Thuringia, to pass the anniversary of her death near her grave; for his love to her was still deep and true, although it soon after ceased to be the one master feeling of his heart

He longed for the affection of a true woman's heart, and the hopes of a home in which he could find rest and peace after his hard practical labours. About this time he won the love of Julie Charpentier, the daughter of the Mine Director. Julie had not only a well-trained mind, but a feeling and tender heart, joined to great grace and beauty. His love for her was not the same passion of devotion he had felt for Sophie, but it was the calm, restful confidence which might last unchanged for a lifetime. Intercourse with her quickened both his heart and his head. Thus his residence at Freiberg offered him additional attraction.

He did not, however, neglect the Muses, and these, his old friends, remained long faithful to him. He composed at this time the following poems: – "Flowers," "Faith and Love; or, The King and Queen," and *Hymns to the Night*, which he published, under the name of "Novalis," in the Prussian *Jahr Buch* (Annual Register), 1798, and *Schlegel's Athenäum*, 1798 and 1800.

It was now time to make some fixed plans for his future life. He wished to live in Thuringia, and to obtain some post which, with a moderate salary, might allow him some leisure for cultivating science, seeing his friends, and enjoying his home.

In 1799 he was appointed Assessor at the Salines, and entrusted with the legal business. At this period he became intimate with Ludwig Tieck, with whom he formed a warm friendship. He consulted him about all his literary work, and passed many happy days with him and Reichardt at Reichardt's country place at Giebichenstein. Part of the winter of 1799 was spent by him at Artem, one of the Salines, and he found there two excellent friends in Major von Funk and Captain Thilemann, both in the Saxon Regiment of Hussars, men of talent and education, acquainted with all the latest works on philosophy and literature. In spite of the time he devoted to them, he did not neglect the salt works, and often while standing apparently lost in dreams, he was thinking out improved processes for technical working. There is little use in asking what he accomplished, one can only surmise what he might have done had he lived to riper years. He was deeply lamented, and the Bergrath Heun frequently said, "No one can ever know what we have lost in him."

In 1800 an Amtmann's place fell vacant in Thuringia. Hardenburg saw in it the completion of his life's plans. It offered him varied work, and many opportunities of usefulness; he could still retain his position at the Salines; and thus his way seemed opening up to claim Julie's hand and enjoy the happiness of a home of his own. It would be a busy life, still he would have sufficient leisure to cultivate both science and literature.

Fortune favoured him. His wish was granted, his examination

successful, and nothing remained but to enter on his new post. Already he had shown signs of great delicacy, when on a journey to Dresden, and the unexpected death of a younger brother had so affected him, as to bring on the rupture of a blood-vessel. He was attended to with loving care by his brothers Carl and Anton, and by Julie, who, at his father's wish, came to them at Dresden. But care and love were all unavailing. He suffered no pain, and said he was only weary, not ill, and in spring he would be himself again.

His last letter to me was dated February 1st, 1801, Weissenfels.

"Again a little friendly word, after such a long pause. Meantime, things have not gone well with me. Now I am better. I am taking a milk cure, nothing else, and it seems to suit me. My father fetched me away from Dresden; I was glad to go, I needed rest and Julie's company. She came here with us, and will stay. I gained some useful experience in Dresden. I cannot write yet, but can read, think, and sympathize. Greet your wife and niece heartily from me. I long to see you, and hear what happens at the Fair. Continue to love me, and think often of your devoted friend."

Though his body was feeble, his mind was active as ever. He read a good deal, especially the *Bible*, Lavater's and Zinzendorf's works, and even worked at his business, and wrote poetry.

He was delighted by a visit from his dear friend SchlegeL Every day they had long talks about their works.

On the 25th of March, as his brother Carl was playing to him some favourite melody, he sank into a calm sleep, from which he never woke in this world. Carl and Schlegel were alone with him.

Who can tell what was the cause of his early death, unless that the active mind had worn out the body? His friends mourned his death, and those who knew his talent deplored it as a great loss to science and mankind.

The strength and clearness of his imagination was his most conspicuous quality, and this made it easy for him to perceive rapidly the scope and bearing of any subject. He called it the chief element of existence, and averred that it was a powerful aid to his religious views.

"I am rejoiced," he wrote to me from Freiberg, 26th December, 1798,

"if my scattered thoughts have occupied a few hours pleasantly – if they have been to you what they were to me – and still are, the commencement of fresh trains of thought, texts for thought. Many are mere fancies of quite transitory value. Others bear the stamp of my deepest convictions. I must confess that I look upon religion from a very different point from you – a point of view which may appear to you both strange and wonderful. At the same time we are friends, and shall remain friends; and here our religion, or rather our theology, touches. If each in its way produces friendship, love, morality, and activity, they must be both sisters, members of that holy family of religions, which from time immemorial have been at home with men, ever preserving, even in the roughest ages, virtue and love, and sheltering under their fostering care, comfort and hope, courage and contentment. Your friend has won your heart by an appeal to your understanding, for reason is the guiding principle of your life; mine has gained me by her genial imagination, which is in accord with the leading feature of my character. Is it not natural that our peculiar and manifold characteristics should show themselves in this most important of all subjects? You rest, with childlike confidence, on the immutable evidence of a mysterious chronicle, which for ages untold has been a palladium to countless multitudes, inspiring them with Divine aspirations – a chronicle which (apart from a few incomprehensible passages) is full of precepts, stories, and teaching which agree in their scope with all the best and wisest of men, and one our consciences have ever considered the best and the truest. Beyond all this, a spiritual world like the vault of heaven is revealed to us by it, which opens out an entrancing view of a heavenly future.

"With what feelings in your heart do you not take the *Bible* in your hand, looking upon it as a pledge of God and eternity; how happy you must seem to yourself to possess a supernatural archive, an open revelation in these pages, which are like a guiding hand from a higher sphere!

"Your theology is the theology of an historical, critical reason, which seeks a firm foundation, an irrefragable evidence, and finds both in a collection of archives whose very existence is in itself a miracle, and whose authenticity is attested not only by history, but by your own heart and reason.

"I rest less on the letter and authenticity of the Scriptures; much less on circumstantial evidence. I am inclined to look within myself for traces of higher influence, and take my own views of primitive times. I look on the Christian religion as the purest model of universal religion, and the most perfectly inspired. But when I say that I trace revelation in every form of theology, and see in them a gradual evolution which runs parallel to the history of civilization, you will say that my imagination is running away with me."

Every year religion became more and more a necessity of his life. A few months before his death, in November, 1800, he wrote,

"Unless bodily illness disturbs me, which does not often happen, my soul is at peace. Religion is the glorious, unclouded Orient. Without it I were miserable. Resting in it, all my thoughts focus in a quiet, ever-living faith."

After Sophie's death, he became devoted to the writings of Lavater and Zinzendorf, various books of Roman Catholic devotion, and even Jacob Boehme's works. Hence the expressions in his hynms which surprise us in so enlightened a thinker. But no one can read his hymn to Jesus,
        "What had I been without Thee?"
without being animated with the most exalted devotion. His hymns were portions of a hymn-book which he and Tieck intended publishing. The modern hymns seemed to him with justice too cold, appealing more to the head than the heart. He considered Gillert's as wanting in imagination. If he gave way too much to that faculty, it must be remembered that they were his first attempts in that kind of composition. After Sophie's death, faith in God and eternity became necessities of his existence, as may have been seen in his letters. Love to Jesus arose later in his heart, and his aesthetic taste led him to very reverential views of the Virgin Mary.

His active fancy saw materials for poetry all around him. All nature was full of poetry to him, and in Jacob Boehme he found the highest poetry. I could not follow him in these flights. Those who appreciate the new poetry will understand him, and see by his *Ofterdingen* what his views were on that point.

His friends Schlegel and Tieck published his writings under the name of "Novalis". It would be doing him great injustice to judge them as if they were finished masterpieces, or a full representation of the real man. He himself looked on literature as a training school. "Authorship," so he wrote to me,

"is a secondary thing. You can judge me more equitably by the chief thing – practical life. If I am good, useful, active, loving, and true, you must make allowance for anything which is useless, untrue, and hard in this sediment The writings of unknown men are harmless, for they are little read and soon forgotten. I treat my writings as a mental education. It teaches me to reflect and work out my own ideas – that is all I expect from it. If I meet the approval of some dear friend, that transcends my fondest expectations. One has to ascend by many steps to a perfect education; one should be tutor, professor, even labourer, as well as writer."

He was gifted with very clear reasoning powers, as well as with strong imagination. How else could he have fathomed all the depths of speculative philosophy? Study with him was a means, not an end. He set bounds to pure speculation, and agreed with Jacobi's letter to Fichte.

"My philosophical books," he wrote to me, in 1800,

"are now at rest in my bookcase. I am thankful to have passed over the high peaks of pure reason, and to have returned to the beautiful land of sense, in which my soul and body live. I rejoice when thinking of my past exertions. They are part of life's training. Reflection and full exercise of the faculties are an absolute necessity. Only one must not forget the writer when poring over the grammar, nor in the arrangement of the letters forget the greatness of the ideas. One may prize philosophy without wishing her for a mistress, and living only for her. Mathematics alone will form neither soldier nor mechanic; philosophy by itself cannot raise to perfect manhood."

To perfect manhood, in the noblest sense of the words, he wished to attain – his calm judgment led him to be absolutely unprejudiced and impartial. He distinguished always between the writer and the man, between both and the friend. The most severe criticism of the author never hurt him, but he could not conceal his annoyance when the attack was personal. The well-known play of Kotzebue's, in which Schlegel was so severely caricatured, did not annoy him, because it was only one author quizzing another, and Schlegel had first thrown down the gauntlet. He admired Schlegel's *Lucinde* as a work of art, but would have blushed to place it in the hand of a young girl. He was pre-eminently sincere – it was so completely woven into the texture of his character that one cannot understand him without recognizing it. It gave dignity to his imagination and reason, and intensified his individuality; it can be traced in all its writings and letters, in his religion and his devotion to parents, brothers and sisters, sweethearts and friends. He found the greatest pleasure in quiet home-life, and was so free from pretension and so unassuming that he seemed created for friendship.

In mixed company among strangers he was often silent for hours, although a keen observer of all that passed; but among friends he was very animated. He felt a necessity for talking out his ideas. One could listen to him evening after evening without ever being wearied, as he had the art of infusing a fresh interest into every subject he handled. In those hours he revealed the richness of his fancy, the sharpness of his reason, and the sincerity of his nature. He was never annoyed by contradiction.

He was tall, well-built, and slight. His eyes betrayed his wit, his mouth his friendly disposition. He was simple in all his tastes, and hated display. He lived in the region of elevated taste, not in that of material pleasure, and the mind was ever the ruler of the body. Thus he created an invisible world in which he lived, while still bound by the flesh. The unseen world was the object of his ceaseless desire, and thither has he been recalled, perfected by life's discipline.

# ILLUSTRATIONS

Novalis

Novalis

Sophie von Kühn

# HEINRICH VON OFTERDINGEN

Heinrich von Ofterdingen was one of the six renowned poets of Germany in the commencement of the thirteenth century, who met in poetical contest at the Court of the Duke of Thuringia. Heinrich Schreiber, Walther von der Vogelweide, Wolfram d'Eschenbach, Reinhart de Zwetzer, and Bittirhoff were nobles; Heinrich von Ofterdingen the son of an Eisenach burgher. The five nobles despised poor Heinrich, who was quite their equal in talent and popularity. According to the tradition, they tried to murder him, and he only escaped by clinging to the folds of the Duchess Sophie's mantle.

At last it was settled that all six should contend for mastery in presence of the Duke and all his Court; the public executioner being present, rope in hand, to hang the one whose songs were deemed the worst.

A crowd of knights and nobles assembled from all parts of Germany to assist at this solemnity.

The poets sang in praise of their favourite princes, about religion, the marriage of the soul, the body after the resurrection, the inexhaustible clemency of God, the power of repentance, the empire of the Cross, and the glories of Mary. (These songs are preserved under the title of the *War of the Wartburg*, which exists at Jena with the contemporary melodies. It was published in 1830.)

As no one could decide on the respective merits of the minstrels, Heinrich von Ofterdingen was sent to Transylvania to fetch the celebrated master Klingsohr, who was so expert in the seven liberal arts, and so versed in astronomy and necromancy, that the spirits were obliged to obey his behests. The King of Hungary paid him a yearly pension of three hundred silver marks for his services. A year was given to Heinrich von Ofterdingen to accomplish his mission, and on the day fixed he returned with the learned man.

Legend repents that Klingsohr and the minstrel were transported during the night by airy sprites to the best hotel at Eisenach, and that Heinrich was much amazed on his awakening to recognize the familiar chimes of St. George.

When Klingsohr came down into the garden towards evening, he was warmly greeted by many of the nobles of Hesse and Thuringia, as well as the Duke's retainers and a number of wealthy burghers. They surrounded him, begging to be told some news. Klingsohr rose, and, after steadfastly gazing at the stars, announced, "I see a lovely star rising over Hungary, which shines on Marbourg, and from thence all over the world. A daughter has just been born to the King of Hungary. She will be named Elizabeth, given in marriage to the eldest son of the Duke of Thuringia. She will be a saint, and renowned all through Christendom."

This news was carried to the Duke, who, next day, as soon as Mass was said, rode down to Eisenach to meet the learned master and escort him to the Wartburg. The greatest honours were shown him, especially by the priests, who treated him as if he were a bishop. Klingsohr presided over the poetic tournament, and succeeded in calming all rivalry.

Vita Rythmica.
*Translator's Note*

# HEINRICH VON OFTERDINGEN

# CHAPTER I

# EXPECTATION

The parents were already asleep, the tall old clock ticked monotonously, the wind sighed through the ill-fitting casements; at times the moon flooded the room with light. The youth tossed on his couch, as he pondered on the stranger's tales.

"It is not the treasures which I care for," he said to himself; "such covetousness is far from me, but I long to see the blue flower. I cannot get rid of the idea, it haunts me. I never felt like this before; it is as if I had dreamed of it long ago, or had had a vision of it in another world; for who would trouble themselves so much about a flower in this world? and I never heard of anyone being in love with a flower. Whence came this stranger? None of us ever saw such a man. I know not why his words impressed me so deeply; the others heard him, and it produced no such effect on their minds. I cannot even express the strange state I am in. Sometimes rapt in delight; but when I forget about the blue flower, a nameless longing takes possession of me; – no one can understand this. I might think I were mad, were it not that my thoughts are so clear and connected, and I understand so many new things. I have heard say that, in the olden days, beasts, rocks, and flowers all spoke to men. I am haunted by the idea that they have something to tell me, and feel as if I could comprehend their speech. Formerly I was devoted to dancing, now I love music."

Gradually the youth lost himself in his sweet fancies, and fell fast asleep. He dreamt of strange, far-off lands, wild, unknown regions. He seemed to float across vast expanses of ocean; he saw marvellous animals; lived with manifold tribes of men, sometimes in scenes of war and riot, sometimes in peaceful huts. He fell into captivity, and suffered cruel privations. Every sensation was quickened to intensity. He lived a life of ever-changing pleasures; died, came alive again; was passionately in love, then separated from her he loved for ever. At last, towards morning, at the break of dawn, calmness stole over him, and his thoughts became more clear and definite. He seemed wandering alone through a gloomy forest. Only an occasional ray of light glinted through the tangled green canopy above him. At length he reached a ravine, up which wound a precipitous path. He scrambled over mossy rocks, the empty bed of a torrent. The higher he went, the less dense was the forest. At last he reached a little meadow on the slope of the hill. Above it towered a cliff, at whose foot he observed a little opening, which led to a rock-hewn passage. He hurried along it for some time till he reached a wider space, guided by a faint, glimmering light. As he entered the grotto he was dazzled by a shaft of light, bright as gold, which sprang up like a fountain, almost touching the high, vaulted roof and showering down innumerable sparks into a great marble basin. Not a sound broke the silence. He approached the basin, which trembled and quivered with every colour of the prism. The walls of the grotto were clothed in light, which diffused a pale-blue lustre, but gave no heat. He dipped his hand in the basin and touched his lips; as he did so, he felt a thrill of energy pervade his whole being. An irresistible impulse led him to undress and bathe in this mystic element. It was a sensation as if of immersion in sunset clouds, indescribable bodily enjoyment, while a rush of quickened thought and feeling called up new and amazing images and pictures, which seemed, as he gazed, no fancy, but reality. The very element which surrounded him grew transformed into beauteous fire-maidens, looking at him with loving eyes. Intoxicated with delight, he swam along the sparkling stream which poured out of the basin through the cavern. Deep, sweet sleep overpowered him. When he woke he was lying on the soft sward of a valley at the edge of a well. At a little distance rose hazy blue cliffs, through whose sides shone gleaming veins of gold. All around him was a soft, mellow light, and the skies above were blue and cloudless. What most attracted him was a lovely blue flower growing at the edge of the well. Its large, glossy, green leaves overshadowed him. The air was perfumed by the fragrance of flowers of every hue, but he cared for none of them but the blue flower, at which he gazed in tender adoration. As he rose to examine it more closely, it seemed to move and change; the glossy leaves hung down by the stalk, and the blossom bent towards him; the petals slowly opened, and he saw a lovely, tender face. Amazed at this unexpected sight, he was about to speak, when he was aroused by his mother's voice, and he found himself in his own room, the golden light of early day streaming through the casement. He had been too happy in his dream to feel irritated at being aroused. He embraced his mother tenderly, wishing her good morning. His father greeted him with reproaches. "You sleepy head! see how you have kept me waiting for breakfast. Here I have been sitting and filing at my work, as the mother forbade my using the hammer lest the dear boy should be disturbed! It is well that you have chosen a learned profession. I have been told that learned doctors have to study half the night."

"Dear father," replied Heinrich, "don't be angry with me for oversleeping myself for once. I was very late in falling asleep, and tossed in restless dreams, until at last I had a dream which I can never forget, and which, indeed, seems more than a mere dream."

"Child," said the mother, "you have been lying on your back, or your thoughts have been astray at evening prayers. You look quite strange. Eat and drink, and cheer up."

The mother went out; the father went on working and grumbling – "Dreams are froth, whatever the highly-learned gentlemen may say, and you ought not to let your mind dwell on such nonsense. The ages are long past since God spoke to men in dreams, and we can neither think nor guess what were the feelings of the chosen few of whom the *Bible* tells us. In those days, human affairs and dreams were in a different phase. In our days there is no open communication with heaven. The old writings are the only sources of our knowledge of the supernatural. Instead of open revelation, the Holy Spirit now influences the intellect of gifted men, and teaches us by the life and actions of good men. I care little about the miracle-working images which the priests tell us about, though I would never laugh at anyone's faith."

"But, dear father, why are you so opposed to dreams, when, by their strange changes and tender influence, they awaken reflection? Is not every dream, even the most confused, a curious cleft in the mysterious curtain which veils our inner life? In the wisest books one finds countless dreams of trustworthy men. Just think of the dream which the Court Chaplain told us the other day, and which appeared to you so remarkable. But, apart from these tales, if you only had one dream in your life, how you would wonder at so unheard-of an occurrence. I think dreams are a relief from the monotony of life, a refreshment for our fancy, they interrupt the serious tenor of life with a little play. Were it not for dreams, we should sooner grow old. And so, without laying too much stress on them, we may look upon them as cheerful companions in life's pilgrimage, from the cradle to the grave. Certainly my last night's dream was no chance occurrence in my life; it was as if a great wheel raised my soul in its tremendous gyrations."

The father smiled cheerfully, and turning to the mother, who just then entered, said, "Mother, Heinrich bears the mark of my own youthful impressions. I was a different man at the time of our marriage. I had just returned from Rome; the warm Southern climate had thawed my Northern nature; I was over-flowing, with fun and spirit, and you were a bright, lovely girl. How well I remember our wedding; it was the gayest ever celebrated at Augsburg, and your father had sent for all the actors and singers from far and near."

"Do you remember telling me in those days of a strange dream you had in Rome," said the mother; "a dream which, you assured me, led you to Augsburg to pay court to me?"

"You recall it to me in the nick of time," replied the father; "I had quite forgotten all about it; but though it made a great impression on me at the moment, it is a proof of the truth of all I have said. No one could have had a more distinct and consecutive dream – even now every incident recurs to me; – but what has it led to? That soon after I longed to see you, and call you mine, was very natural, as I knew you well. I had been struck at first sight by your sweet, cheerful nature, only my longing for distant scenes had prevented my making love to you. When the dream occurred, I was wearied of travel and longing for a home."

"Father, do tell me your dream."

"One evening," said the father, "I felt sad and home-sick; and, leaving my noisy companions, strolled out under the deep-blue sky, amid old ruins and pillars, which looked weird and ghostly in the pale light of the moon. Feeling thirsty, I went up to a large country house to ask for a drink of milk. An old man came out, and looked suspiciously at me. I made my request; and when he saw that I was a stranger, and a German, he kindly asked me into his study, and set a bottle of wine before me. He made me sit down, and asked me what my profession was. The room was full of books and antiquities. We entered into conversation, and he told me much that was interesting about olden times, poets, sculptors, and artists. I felt as though in a new sphere. He showed me cameos, seals, and other works of art; then read some poems with marvellous fire and emphasis. It warms my heart even now to think of the talk, which lasted far into the night. At last he showed me to a bedroom, as it was too late to return to town. I soon fell asleep, and dreamt that I was standing at the gate of my father's town. I felt as if I was bound on some important errand, but could not recall what it was. On I went towards the Harz Mountains. I was gay and light-hearted, as if at a wedding, as I hurried up hill and down dale, through woods and meadows, till I reached the top of a high mountain. Below flowed the golden Aue, and fair Thuringia lay stretched at my feet. Opposite me was the noble range of the Harz, with countless castles, convents, and farms nestling amid the woods. Presently I perceived a stair cut in the rock, down which I took my way. In a short time I reached a grotto. There sat an old man, in flowing robes, absorbed in contemplation of a beautiful maiden sculptured in whitest marble. The old man's beard swept the ground. He looked grave, yet friendly, much like one of the works of art I had been looking at during the evening. The cavern was full of light. As I stood gazing at the old hermit, my host tapped me on the shoulder, grasped my hand, and led me down long, gloomy passages. After a while I saw a light, and hastened towards it. Soon I found myself in a luxuriant meadow; but all around me was far different from Thuringia. Gigantic trees, with large, glossy leaves, cast a deep shadow on the ground. The air was hot, but not oppressive. There were flowers and streams in all directions; and amongst all the flowers, one particularly charmed me."

"Oh, dearest father, tell me what was its colour?" asked Heinrich, excitedly.

"I cannot remember."

"Was it blue?"

"Maybe," continued the father, without noticing Heinrich's emotion; "but I do know that it awoke inexpressible sensations in my mind. I turned round, and saw my guide smiling at me. What happened next I do not clearly remember. Again we stood on a hill; my guide stood by me. 'You have seen the wonder of the world,' he said. 'It depends upon yourself to be the happiest man on earth, and to attain celebrity. Heed my words. If you return hither on the eve of St. John, and pray to God to enlighten you as to the dream, you may have the highest earthly life. Mark a little blue flower which you will see on your way. Pluck it, and await humbly Divine guidance. Then my dream led me among the noblest forms of men, and endless ages passed with their bewildering changes before my eyes. My tongue seemed unloosed. What I said sounded like sweetest music. Then I looked up and saw your mother, with a friendly, blushing face. She held a beauteous child in her arms, which she placed in mine. The child seemed suddenly to grow and expand. A dazzling light environed it as it unfolded snow-white wings and rose into the air, holding us in its arms. It flew and soared higher and higher, till the earth lay beneath us like a golden ball. I woke, took a friendly farewell of my kind host, who begged me to return. I should have done so, but a sudden impulse made me leave Rome, and hurry home to Augsburg as I longed intensely to meet your mother."

# CHAPTER II

St. John's Day was long past and gone, when the mother consented to go to her father in Augsburg, and show him his unknown but much-loved grandson.

Some merchants, friends of Ofterdingen, were going there on business, and promised a safe convoy. The mother was the more pleased to go, because she had noticed that for some time past her boy had been more quiet and reflective than usual. She thought he was melancholy or ill, and that a long journey, the sight of new countries, mixing with fresh acquaintances, and perhaps falling in love with one of her pretty countrywomen, would drive away his gloom, and make him as sympathetic and cheerful as before. The old man agreed to the plan, and Heinrich was rejoiced at the notion of seeing a country the theme of so many of his mother's stories, and which he had long dreamt of as an earthly paradise.

Heinrich was just twenty years old. As yet he had never left the neighbourhood of his father's town. He only knew the world by hearsay. He had seen but few books. The household of a Graf was very simple and quiet, as in those times even a prince's establishment was far inferior in splendour and comfort to the home of a private gentlemen in modern days. For that very reason the people prized all their possessions highly. The art and skill shown in their production, added to the interest inspired by their having been handed down generation after generation, made them almost sacred heirlooms. They were often looked upon as pledges for the happiness and prosperity of a large family, whose fate was inextricably connected with theirs.

A picturesque poverty showed off to more advantage the few carefully-guarded treasures dimly seen in the dusky halls inhabited by our ancestors. If it is true that a careful distribution of light, colour, and shade is needful to bring out the hidden beauties of the visible world, so in those days the same thrifty distribution was apparent in the household; far different from the luxury and superabundance of ornament in our modern dwellings, which produce no effect but commonplace monotony.

Between the times of rough barbarism and the present age of knowledge and art, a transition period existed, an age of thought and romance. Who does not love to wander in the twilight, when night gives way to dawn, and the light breaks down the shadows of the night with a glow of gorgeous colour? In the same way we love to retrace the age in which Heinrich lived, when all was fresh and new to heart and intellect.

He took leave of his comrades and his teacher, the wise old Court Chaplain, who dismissed his gifted pupil with a blessing. The Landgrävin was his godmother; he had often been to see her at the Wartburg; he went to bid her farewell, and received much good advice, and a golden chain.

Heinrich was sad when he left his home; for the first time he realized what separation meant. He had not felt it when preparing to go, it was only at the moment of parting that his former life seemed torn away from him, and he seemed entering upon a new phase of existence. The first parting is like the first death: a bitter experience of changing in time, when earthly joys fade, we deem both but reminders of another world, where all is certain and enduring. His mother's presence comforted the youth; the old state of things had not completely deserted him.

It was early dawn when the travellers passed through the gates of Eisenach. As it grew brighter and clearer, Heinrich observed the new, unknown region through which they travelled. At last they reached a rising ground, which offered them a farewell glance of home. The sun shone brightly on the forsaken valley, and old thoughts and memories crowded on Heinrich's recollection. He was now on the the summit of the range he had so often longed to reach, and of which fancy had drawn such marvellous pictures. The wonder-blossom was beckoning him on and on, and as he cast a lingering glance on fair Thuringia, he wondered when and how he should return to her. The party, until then lost in their own thoughts, now woke up, and made the time pass merrily with talk and stories. Heinrich's mother described the merry life in Suabia in her father's house; the merchants chimed in, praising old Schwaning's hospitality, and speaking warmly of the beauty of the Suabian maidens. "You do well," they said to Heinrich's mother, "to take your son there; manners are gentler in Suabia than elsewhere. They do not neglect what is useful, but they love what is ornamental. They carry out their work with a daintiness and care unknown elsewhere. There the merchant is honoured, and grows wealthy. Arts and handicrafts increase, and are more considered; the work seems lighter to the artisan, because it ensures him manifold comforts, as good work commands good pay. Trade increases, the country advances in prosperity, and new towns spring into existence. The more the daytime business, the more enjoyable become evenings consecrated to amusement and the arts. The mind longs for rest and variety. In no other country are there more charming singers, graceful dancers, and glorious artists. The neighbourhood of Italy softens the manners and enlarges the scope of conversation. The ladies adorn all social gatherings; nor need they fear remark, if they prove their talent by emulating the mental activity of the men. The solemn gravity or wild frolics of the men are exchanged for cheerful animation and gentle gaiety: friendship and love are the guiding spirits of these pleasant meetings. Nowhere are more blameless maidens and truer wives than in Suabia.

"Yes, young friend, you will lose your timidity in the bright, warm air of southern Germany; the pretty girls will soon loosen your tongue. The fact of your being a stranger and a grandson of old Schwaning, who is the mainspring of society, will attract all eyes to you. I do not doubt we shall see you bring home a Suabian bride, as your father did."

Heinrich's mother, with a happy blush, thanked the merchants for speaking so well of her fatherland. "Even if you do not devote yourself to art, like your father," continued one of the merchants, "and prefer a learned profession, you need not become a priest, and renounce all the deepest joys of life. It is wrong that science should be exclusively in the hands of men who are debarred from practical life, and that princes seek as their prime advisers such unsociable and inexperienced persons. In Suabia you will find clever and experienced laymen; choose whichever branch of learning you like, and you will find plenty of teachers."

Heinrich, who had been thinking of his friend the Court Chaplain, here interrupted the speaker: "My ignorance of the world does not allow me to contradict your theory; but I must remind you of our good old friend, the Chaplain, who is a model of a wise man, and to whose advice and teaching I owe much."

"We honour this excellent man with all our hearts," replied the merchant; "and give him all praise for his conduct, which is, in all respects, pleasing to God; but allow us to differ from you as regards general knowledge, for he is so absorbed in spiritual lore that he has no insight or penetration in worldly matters." "But," said Heinrich, "should not this higher knowledge make a man more capable of managing earthly affairs? Is not childish simplicity a safer guide through the labyrinth of this world than selfish cleverness, which is led astray and dazzled by innumerable complications? I may be wrong, but it seems to me as if there were two paths by which one may attain knowledge of human life: one difficult and interminable, with countless turns and twists, the path of experience; the other, which reaches the goal in one bound, the way of inward reflection. Forgive me, if I speak of my childish fancies; only confidence in your kindness, and the thought of my old teacher who instructed me in the better way, has made me so bold."

"We must confess that we cannot follow your reasoning, but we honour you for your warm affection for your good master. You seem to have the mind of a poet; you speak so fluently, and your expressions and comparisons are so choice. Also you have a leaning to the marvellous, which is the province of the poet."

"I do not know," said Heinrich. "I have often heard of poets and singers, but I have never met any. I cannot even form an idea of their strange art. I long to meet them, for then I think I could better understand it. I have often heard of poetry, but I have never seen any, and I could not understand what my teacher told me about it. He said it was a noble art, and one to which I would devote myself if I learned it. In olden days it was much more common than now; every one knew somewhat of it. It has been lost, as well as many allied arts. The singers honoured God, they were inspired from on high, and taught heavenly wisdom in fascinating measures." "We have never troubled ourselves about poetry," said the merchants, "though we have often heard songs with pleasure. No doubt a poet is born under a peculiar star; it is a wonderful art, and quite different from all others. Poetry and painting can be acquired by diligence and patience. The harmony is in the strings, it only needs to be evoked. In painting, Nature herself is the teacher. She produces innumerable, wonderful figures, gives light and shade, so that a skilful hand, a quick eye, and experience in the mixing of colours, render it possible to imitate her. It is easy to understand how fascinating this art must be. The nightingale's song, the sighing of the wind, beautiful forms, lights, colours, please us because they occupy our sense in an agreeable manner. But Poetry is quite apart from this. She has no tools, no handicraft, the eye and the ear give no help, for this noble art does not come by hearing: it is all inward. Just as artists are swayed by pleasant sensations, so the soul of the poet is permeated, consecrated by high and noble thoughts. He knows

* 69

how to excite our noblest feelings; he transports us into a new and marvellous world. The past and the future are evoked; countless characters, magic landscapes, strange events are marshalled before us, and shut out the well-known present. One hears strange words, and knows not what they mean. The poet's periods fascinate; even common expressions have a borrowed charm which bewitch the hearer."

"You excite my curiosity still more," said Heinrich. "Tell me, I beg you, about the singers you have heard. I can remember enough of these strange beings; I feel as if I had heard of them in my early youth; but what you say is so clear and distinct, that I realize their power for the first time."

"We have passed many happy hours in Italy, France, and Suabia in the company of singers, and rejoice that what we have said has interested you. When one is travelling thus among the mountains, pleasant converse beguiles the weary way. Perhaps it might please you to hear some stories about poets which we have heard in our journeys. Of the songs themselves we can tell but little. The joy and the excitement which they create prevent one remembering the mere words, and ceaseless business blunts the memory.

"In olden times, all nature was more animated than now. Wise men could then achieve things which now seem fabulous and impossible. We have heard that in past ages there were poets among the Greeks who could charm into life the spirits of the woods, call up blooming gardens in the desert, tame wild beasts, calm the wildest tribes, and accustom them to law and order and the enjoyment of the arts of peace, change roaring torrents into placid streams, and excite even the stones to the rhythmic measures of the dance. They were prophets and priests, law-givers and physicians; taught the deepest lore, and could discern the secrets of the future – the secret nature of all things; the virtues and healing powers in numbers, herbs, and all creatures. They reduced nature to fixed laws. Strange is it that so noble an art should have so utterly vanished. It is said that one of these gifted men, a poet, wished to travel in distant lands. He was rich in jewels, the offerings of the grateful. Embarking on board a ship in the bay, he was at first treated by the sailors with all respect, until their covetousness being excited by his treasures, they plotted to throw him overboard and divide his possessions. He offered all his treasures as a ransom, and foretold terrible misfortunes if they carried out their evil intentions: but in vain. When he saw that he could not move them, he begged them to allow him at least to play once before his death, his swan's song, then he would willingly plunge into the ocean with his wooden flute. They knew well that if they granted this request, he would so move their hearts that they could not carry out their wicked plan; but they acceded, and stopped their ears so as to prevent themselves hearing his melody.

"The whole ship echoed his song; the waves chimed in. The sun and stars appeared in the skies, and thousands of fishes leapt in the green waters round the vessel. The sailors stood apart with deaf ears, waiting impatiently for the ending of the song. It was soon over. Then the singer, with a cheerful countenance, plunged into the waters, holding in his hand his wonder-working flute. Scarcely had he touched the sea, when the broad back of a grateful dolphin rose up under him, and bore the astonished poet safely away. In a short time it reached the shore, and gently landed him on a sandy beach. The poet sang a merry song to his deliverer, and went his way. Some time after, as he was walking by the sea-side mourning his lost treasures, the remembrance of happy hours, the tokens of love and friendship, his old friend the dolphin reappeared, and cast on the shore the stolen jewels. After the poet's disappearance, the sailors had quarrelled over the division of the booty, ending in so fierce a struggle that many were killed. The few who remained were unable to manage the ship, so it drifted on a rock and went to pieces. A few struggled to shore, with tattered clothes and empty hands, while the faithful dolphin restored the treasure to its rightful owner."

# CHAPTER III

AFTER a pause, another merchant volunteered to tell a tale.

"It is not so wonderful, and belongs to later days; yet it will please you and instruct you in the power of that strange art. There was an aged King, who lived surrounded by splendour. Far and near people flocked to see his magnificence, and there was no lack of perpetual amusements, dainty banquets, gorgeous decorations, fine fashions, plays, and dances, nor of learned men whose conversation was a feast for the mind, nor of beautiful youths and maidens who were the animating soul of the whole. The old King, who was a stern and serious man, had two motives in all this display. One was his tender devotion to his only daughter (all that remained to remind him of his young wife), a charming and lovable girl, at whose feet he would gladly have laid all the treasures of earth and heaven; the other was a perfect devotion to poetry and poets. From his youth he had been devoted to this art, and had spent vast sums of money in collecting the works of poets of all ages and climes. He attracted poets to his Court from all the ends of the earth, and overwhelmed them with honours. He never wearied of listening to their songs, and would often forget the most pressing business in his enjoyment of a new poem. His daughter had grown up amid poetry and song. Her whole being was like a tender poem, an expression of sadness and longing. The beneficent effects of poetry were seen all through the land, especially at Court. Life was all the more enjoyable because poetry banished all low, mean passions, which, like discords, vanished in the presence of the pure harmony of enlightened souls. In those happy days peace of mind and holy contemplation were the lot of all. Jealousy was only known in the old legends, where it was spoken of as the enemy of mankind. It seemed as if the Spirit of Poetry had rewarded the old King by imbuing his daughter with every lovable gift. When she appeared at the feasts, surrounded by a band of graceful maidens all arrayed in white, to listen to the friendly contests of the poets, and blushingly crowned the victor with a garland of sweetest flowers, she might have been taken for the embodiment of the sacred art.

"One sorrow alone disturbed this earthly paradise. The King grew daily older, and yet there seemed no prospect of a suitable marriage being arranged for the Princess. No subject could dare to raise his eyes to so perfect a creature, they looked upon her as a supernatural being; and the princes from foreign lands, who had been attracted by her beauty, seemed all too unworthy of such a prize. The culture of the Court repelled them, and soon it was rumoured everywhere that this royal family was so proud and high-minded that no prince could endure to be brought in contact with it. This rumour was not altogether unfounded. The King was descended from an ancient Eastern dynasty; his wife had been the last descendant of the celebrated warrior Rustum. His poets sounded the praise of his ancestors, the divine rulers of the universe; and in their magic utterances he perceived clearly how high he was placed above other kings. In vain he looked for another Rustum for a son-in-law, as he knew full well that the safety of his realm and the happiness of his subjects called for the marriage of his daughter.

"There lived not far from his capital an old man, who, living on a secluded property, devoted himself to the education of his only son; his only other interest was giving advice to his poor neighbours in cases of illness and sorrow. The youth was grave and studious, devoted to nature, and the sciences which his father taught him. The old man had many years before migrated from distant lands into this blooming country, to enjoy the peace and prosperity which was the result of the King's wise government. He made use of his leisure to search out the secrets of nature, and share his accumulated knowledge with his son. At first sight there was nothing striking in the youth's appearance, except the intelligence of his eyes; but the more one looked at him, the more attractive he became; and when one heard his sweet, melodious voice discoursing on rare and hidden mysteries, he exercised a positive fascination.

"One day the Princess had ridden alone in the forest to enjoy absolute freedom of thought, and to learn some new and beautiful poem. The coolness of the forest tempted her on and on, until she reached the secluded house where the old man lived. Dismounting from her horse, she fastened it to a tree, and going up to the door asked for a glass of milk. The youth started at the sight of the enchanting maiden, whose majestic bearing had all the attraction of youth and beauty, together with the tender grace of a pure and noble soul. While he hastened to fulfil her wish, his father invited his guest to enter the house, and take a seat by the hearth, from which rose a light blue noiseless flame. At her entrance she was struck by a thousand unaccustomed objects, as well as by the order and beauty of the whole. A sacred influence seemed to pervade the building, an impression heightened by the simple robes of the venerable old man and the modest dignity of his son. The old man guessed from her rich and tasteful dress that she belonged to the Court. During the youth's absence, she asked about some curiosities, especially some strange pictures placed near the hearth, which the old man explained clearly and attractively.

"Soon the son returned with a jug of new milk, which he offered in an unaffected and respectful manner.

"After some agreeable discourse, the Princess thanked them heartily for their hospitality; and, blushing, requested permission to come again to hear more about the wonderful curiosities which had so excited her interest. She then rode off, without betraying her rank, as she saw neither father nor son guessed who she was. In spite of their neighbourhood to the capital, neither of them had ever cared to join in the Court festivities. They were absorbed in their own pursuits, and satisfied with each other's society. The youth never cared to leave his father, save for an hour or two, when he searched the forest for butterflies, rare insects, and plants.

"This chance meeting was a momentous one for both youth and maiden. The old man soon saw the deep impression which the stranger had made on his son. His youth and his tender heart made his first love all the stronger. The old man had long foreseen such a possibility, and felt sympathy with his son when he thought of their lovely and unexpected guest.

"The Princess felt a new sensation in the heart as she rode home. She foresaw the dawning of a new untried world. A magic veil seemed to shroud her clear perception, and she fancied she must have entered some supernatural world. Poetry, which formerly had occupied her whole soul, seemed now a feint echo of distant times. On her return to the palace, she shrank from its splendour and magnificence, and felt ill at ease when her father welcomed her. She could not tell him of her adventure, but every one was too used to her absence of mind and moods of abstraction to pay much attention. She was no longer full of spirit, every one around seemed strange, and an unknown depression weighed upon her, until a poet sang a song in praise of hope – setting forth the miracles of faith, which brought about the accomplishment of the heart's desires. This comforted her, and she fell asleep, soothed by the sweetest dreams.

"After taking leave of the Princess, the youth, who had followed her unseen to the palace, wandered for hours in the depths of the forest. On his way home he saw something bright lying in the path. He stooped to pick it up, and found it was a dark-red gem which sparkled on one side and bore mysterious characters on the reverse. It was a large carbuncle, and he remembered seeing it in the lovely maiden's necklace. He hurried home and showed it to his father. They settled that it were best for the youth to see next morning if any messengers were looking for it in the forest; but if not, to keep it till the lovely lady came to reclaim it herself. All night the youth looked at the dazzling gem, and when morning broke he wrote the following lines on the paper in which he wrapped it: –

"Deep in this gem do mystic letters glow;
Deep in my heart a hidden love does grow.
From one there rises sparks of unknown fire,
The other is consumed with love's desire;
In one the glorious light is buried deep,
The other will love's impress ever keep."

"At the first streak of dawn he bent his way to the palace garden.

"In the meantime, the Princess had discovered her loss. The precious stone was a talisman which she had inherited from her mother, and which, as long as she wore it, preserved her from all human influence.

"This loss surprised more than it alarmed her. On reflection, she remembered wearing it the previous day, and never doubted that she had either lost it in the old man's house, or on the forest path. She determined to rise early to seek for it.

"Early in the morning she passed through the garden, and went out into the forest. As she walked faster than usual, it seemed quite natural that her heart should beat quickly.

"The sun rose, gilding the tips of the large forest trees, which rustled and quivered as if greeting its beams. Just then a slight noise in the bushes startled the Princess, and, looking round, she saw the youth.

"Motionless with surprise at the lovely apparition, he stood speechless. At last they greeted one another with all the cordiality of old friends. Before the Princess could explain the cause of her early walk, he handed her the precious talisman with flushed cheeks and a beating heart. She took it silently in a trembling hand, and as a guerdon threw a gold chain over his neck. He knelt at her feet in speechless delight, and she took leave of him with gracious words of thanks, promising to come soon again to see his father's strange and curious collection. The youth bowed respectfully, and watched her retreating form till lost to sight. She soon repeated her visit, and scarcely a morning passed that the youth did not meet at the garden gate and accompany her on long rambles in the forest glades. She kept her birth and rank a perfect secret, it seemed as though she dreaded the result of letting it be known. The youth grew daily more deeply in love with her. He and his father looked upon her as some noble damsel attached to the Court. She showed the old man the affection of a daughter, and soon felt at home in the wonderful house in the forest. At times she brought her lute, and sang divinely to the old man, while the youth lay at her feet drinking in the heavenly tones of her voice. In return he taught her many secrets of nature; he told her how the world had been created by a wondrous action of sympathy, and how the stars joined together in harmonious motion. She was delighted with all he taught her, still more with the facility with which he learned to play her lute to accompany his poetical improvisations.

"They were returning home one day, when his words touched her more deeply than usual. Drawn together by sudden attraction, they exchanged the first kiss. At that moment a terrific clap of thunder broke overhead, and seemed to echo round and round among the forest glades. Threatening clouds swept up from the horizon, and blotted out the light of day. The youth's first thought was to obtain shelter for his lovely companion. Hurrying through the trees, he soon saw that in the gathering darkness he had lost his way. He was overpowered with anxiety; nor was the Princess less disturbed as she thought of her father's dismay when her absence was discovered. Only the loving words of the youth sustained her courage. At last, by a vivid flash of lightning, they perceived the opening into a cavern on a steep hillside. There they hoped to find shelter from the storm, and a place of rest and safety. Fortune favoured them. The cavern was lofty and dry, carpeted with soft green moss. The youth quickly lighted a fire of brushwood, by which they could dry their streaming garments. Here they were safe, secluded from the world, and sheltered from the roar of the elements. A wild almond tree overhung the entrance to the cave; a rippling brook ran close by, at which they could slake their thirst. The youth, who carried the Princess's lute, now struck some chords; and, sitting down by the crackling fire, sang to her song after song, describing his love and adoration. No beings were ever happier, they forgot the world, and all but their mutual love.

"At dawn the storm was over, and in the pure light of day a thousand perplexities beset the poor Princess! The youth cheered her, assuring her of his undying love and devotion. She was comforted, and told him her anxiety arose from her dread of her father's pride, and the grief he must be already enduring. They determined to take counsel with the old man, and the youth sped on his way, promising to return ere long. He soon reached his father's house, and was joyfully received. After deep deliberation on the subject of the lovers, he proposed to conduct the Princess to some subterranean rooms beneath his house, which were so skilfully arranged that they were absolutely undiscoverable. When twilight fell, the youth led her to his father home, where she was most lovingly received. At times she wept when she thought of her father's sorrowing heart, but she hid her grief from her lover, and only confided in his father, who prophesied that all would be well.

"In the meantime, the Court was in dismay when evening came, and the Princess was nowhere to be found. The King sent messengers in all directions. No one could explain the mysterious disappearance. As for an elopement, it never occurred to anyone; for there was no one whom the Princess had ever been seen to favour. The messengers returned one after another with the same hopeless tale, and the King sank into despairing melancholy.

Only when his singers surrounded him at night and sang of hope, he took courage and believed that some day his adored daughter would return. But as soon as he was again alone, his sorrow overwhelmed him, and he wept aloud. Then he thought, 'Of what avail my grandeur and my rank? I am more miserable than man ever was. Nothing can replace my daughter. Without her, even song is but empty words and delusion. It was she who lent enchantment to the song, and gave it form and life. Would I were the meanest of my own subjects, and had my daughter back again. It is not the crown and sceptre which makes the king – it is the feeling of complete satisfaction, the plenitude of earthly joy, the sensation of superabundant possessions. Now my pride is punished; the loss of my wife did not shake it – and now I am condemned to endless woe.' Thus did the poor old King mourn. At times his old pride and severity were more apparent than ever. He scorned complaint, he would suffer in silence and patience as beseemed a king.

"He was convinced that no one had ever known such sorrow as his. When he wandered in the gathering gloom into his daughter's apartments, and saw all her treasured possessions lying about as she left them, grief overpowered him, and he was willing to accept the compassion of the meanest of his household.

"All the citizens and his subjects mourned for him; but there was a secret belief that the Princess was alive, and would come back some day. So passed many months, and spring returned. 'Now the Princess will come, too,' passed from mouth to mouth. Even the King grew more cheerful and hopeful. The former festivities were resumed, and only the Princess was lacking to complete the glory of the Court. One evening, on the anniversary of her disappearance, a brilliant assembly was gathered in the garden. The air was soft and warm, a slight breeze rustled amid the branches of the old trees, as if announcing a welcome message. A fountain rose to a stupendous height, reflecting innumerable lights and torches, and its splashing waters formed a harmonious accompaniment to the music and song which resounded under the lofty trees. The King was seated on a gorgeous carpet, surrounded by courtiers in festal robes. The garden was thronged. Amid the merry groups sat the old King, lost in silence and thought. A vision of his lost daughter rose clearly before him, as he pondered over the happy days which had come to so cruel a close one year ago. Grief and longing overpowered him, and hot tears rolled down his furrowed cheeks. The past year seemed like a cruel nightmare; and as he raised his eyes he fancied he must again behold the much-loved form. The poets had just ceased their recitations, and a deep silence and emotion fell on all, for the last poet had sung of the joys of meeting again, the glory of spring which spoke of never-ending hope.

"Suddenly the silence was broken by a light touch on a lute; and a rich, melodious voice rose at a little distance, under a wide-spreading oak.

"All eyes turned in that direction, and perceived a youth clad in a foreign dress, simple and graceful, holding in his hand a lute. He continued his song; when the King turned to listen, he bowed deeply. The voice was extraordinarily beautiful, the song still more so. He sang of the creation of the world, the beginning of the stars, plants, animals, and men, of the long-forgotten golden days when love and poetry were lords of all. Then he described the advent of hate and cruelty, their ceaseless strife with love; ending in the triumph of love over all, the end of sorrow, the return of the Golden Age, and the restoration of nature to never-ending youth and beauty.

"The poets drew nearer to the youth, impressed with the beauty of his song. All present were thrilled with new-born delight, and the King was overpowered with enthusiasm and heavenly calm. Such a song had never been heard. All thought the youth some supernatural visitant, especially as they marked the beauty of his countenance, and listened to his marvellous accents. As he played, the breeze stirred his long golden locks, the lute seemed animated with fresh life, and his soft deep eyes gazed into a hidden world. Even the calm innocence of his expression denoted no mortal man. At last the glorious melody ceased. The most aged of the poets pressed the youthful singer to his heart, with eyes glistening with tears of joy. A murmur of applause rose among the entranced audience. The King came forward to greet the minstrel, who flung himself at his feet. The King raised him, and bid him ask a boon. He begged permission to sing another song: it was granted. The King withdrew a few paces, and the youth began.

"O'er bogs and fells, as on he roams,
  None heed the lonely bard,
Closed are to him both hearts and homes.
  His life is rough and hard.

"Sad is the lot which is my share,
  All lone I wander here;
Joy give I others, while fell Care
  Her mantle throws o'er me.
The lives of others brightened seem
  By my sweet art and songs;
Yet no true living love they deem
  To poet's work belongs.

"With heart unmoved, they say farewell,
  Nor heed my going more than Spring's;
None mourn the blossoms, for they tell
  Of the rich fruitage Summer brings.
Like vernal blossom, I'm forgot,
  Or as in harvest, golden seed,
I sing of Heaven, their glorious lot –
  Neglect and scorn are all my meed.

"I feel an unseen magic power
  Pour glowing numbers from my tongue;
And long that in some happy hour
  Some heart may by my grief be wrung;
But none, alas! the poet heed,
  No gentle tears for him are shed,
No kindred heart for him does bleed,
  He sings of joy – his joys are dead!

✳ 81

"Upon the sward the poet fell,
  With weary heart and tear-dimmed eyes;
And while he slept a heavenly spell
  Calmed his hot heart and stilled his sighs.
Forget thy woes, the scorn, the strife.
  Throw off the weary weight of care;
Before thee dawns a happier life,
  And royal honours greet thee there."

"The poet stopped, amazement could be seen on every face. During the song, an old man, leading a veiled figure, which bore in its arms a smiling cherub, came forward from behind the singer. The babe held out its dimpled hands to the King, and laughed merrily at the assembled courtiers. The general surprise was increased when the King's tame eagle, which was ever by his side, flew down to the poet, and placed a golden circlet on his brow. The stranger started, and the bird, leaving the diadem on his flowing locks, returned to the King. Giving it to the child, who stretched out his hand to take it, the poet, kneeling on one knee before the monarch, continued, with deepest pathos: –

"The dream that hushed his sorrows fled:
  The poet woke to life's dull care.
With hasty step he onward sped,
  Until he reached a palace fair.
He tunes his lute and sings of love;
  The Princess at her casement hears;
His sad complaint her heart doth move,
  She hurries down to soothe his fears.

"'Tis love that binds so fast their hearts,
  Draws each to each with sudden fire;
Love with its joys, its fears, its smarts,
  For much she dreads her royal sire.
They hide apart in lonely grove.
  Lest pride should break their holy bond;
There live in peace, and joy, and love,
  Yet still the Princess does despond.

"The poet sang to cheer his bride.
  He sang of fortune's speedy dawn.

The old King who that way did ride
  Was by the touching music drawn.
He sees his lovely daughter clasp
  A blue-eyed babe with golden hair;
She hastes to place it in his arms.
  And prays for pardon then and there,

"The poet's lay his pride doth break.
  And change his grief to fervent joy.
Love now restores what love did take,
  And blots away all past annoy.

"Spirit of Song, on us descend,
  Oh, help thou those who to thee cry!
A father's heart to mercy bend.
  That he may list a daughter's sigh,
And, pardoning, clasp her to his heart;
  Then take his grandson in his arms,
Forgive the wandering poet's part,
  And put to flight his wild alarms."

"At the concluding lines the singer withdrew the veil in which the slight woman's form was wrapped. The Princess fell sobbing at her father's feet, holding up the lovely babe. Beside her knelt the youth.

"A breathless pause ensued. For a few moments the King remained grave and silent; then he pressed his daughter to his heart, and wept aloud. He then raised up the kneeling youth, and embraced him tenderly. A hearty cheer rose from the assembly. The King then took the child in his arms, and held it aloft to heaven with a touching air of devotion; then he welcomed the old man. Tears of joy stood in every eye at this moving spectacle. The poets celebrated the occasion in glowing verse, and this auspicious evening was but the foretaste of the peace and joy which overspread the whole country.

"This happy land has vanished. Old legends only record that Atlantis was swallowed by the sea."

# CHAPTER IV

A FEW days passed of uninterrupted travel. The roads were firm and dry, the weather bright and cheering, the region through which they passed fruitful, well populated, and picturesque. The gloomy forest of Thuringia lay behind them. The merchants, who had often travelled that way, had friends everywhere, who received them with cordial hospitality. They avoided lonely places in case of robber bands; and when obliged to pass through such dangerous regions, took a numerous convoy. Some of the owners of mountain castles were on good terms with the merchants, who rode up to them and asked if they had any commissions for Augsburg. A friendly reception was always given to them; and the wives and daughters greeted the strangers also with mingled curiosity and kindness. They were delighted to meet a woman from a town and learn the last fashions in dress, and the newest way of preparing some dainty dish. Both knights and ladies praised young Ofterdingen's mild and winning manners; the latter especially admired his handsome face, which, like a beautiful bud, gave promise of rare excellence.

At one of these castles, where they arrived at nightfall, a jolly party was assembled. The knight was an old soldier, who was never happy unless the monotony of his lonely life was broken by banquets and festivities. He received the travellers with brotherly warmth, and led them to his noisy guests in the great banqueting hall. The mother was put under the care of the lady of the castle. The merchants and Heinrich took their place at the long oaken board, where the cup was circulating freely. Heinrich was excused much drinking on account of his youth, but the merchants were quite ready to do justice to the noble wine. The conversation turned on the chances of war, and Heinrich listened eagerly to tales of the Holy Land, the miracles performed at the Holy Sepulchre, the adventures of the Crusaders by sea and land, their fierce onslaughts on the Saracens, and their life in camp and field. They expressed burning wrath at the Saracens still defiling the holy ground of Palestine, and praised the noble heroes who had gained an immortal crown in their strife with the unbelievers.

The master of the castle showed the richly mounted sword which he had won in a battle from a Saracen whom he killed, whose castle he had burned, and whose wife and children he had taken prisoners. The Emperor, as a reward, had allowed him to quarter a Saracen's head on his shield.

All admired the splendid sword. Henry took it in his hand, and felt seized with a sudden warlike ardour. He kissed it with deepest reverence. This pleased the knight, who embraced him, and urged on him the duty of helping to deliver the Holy City.

"Consider the matter carefully, my son," said the old knight, "a new crusade is about to begin. The Emperor himself will lead us to the East. All hearts are stirring, and all through Europe crowds are hastening to take the Cross. Who knows whether in another year we may not enter Jerusalem as joyful victors, and you and I may feast together, and think of the old fatherland, and the happy meeting which led you, too, to join the conquerors. You may meet some Eastern maiden, too, who may enslave your heart; for their beauty is rare indeed; and after such a conquest there will be hosts of prisoners."

The knights then sang a chorus, which was then the rallying cry of Europe.

"The heathen hold the Holy Grave,
The tomb wherein the Saviour lay,
They gibe, and curse, they mock, and rave
At Him who rose on Easter Day.
Ah! hear the voice which seems to call,
'Up! Christians, up! free it from thrall!'

"There passes over land and ocean,
In silent night, a raging storm,
Which stirs in sleepers new emotion
To bear no more the heathen's scorn.
A voice resounds o'er land and sea,
'Up, Christians, up! and fight for Me!'

"High waves the banner in the air.
And crowds of warriors gather round,
All long and yearn to hasten where
They may set free the sacred ground.
E'en children come, a joyous band,
To share in freeing Holy Land.

"Christians to arms! God's host above
Will watch your dangers, aid your strife;
Fear naught, go forward in His love
Who bids you grudge nor ease nor life,
So that you win from pagan hand
Christ's sepulchre in Holy Land."

Heinrich's whole soul was on fire. The grave in the far-off land
seemed, to his excited imagination, like a beautiful, unprotected
maiden in the hand of an infuriated mob.

Just then his mother sent for him to present him to the noble
Châtelaine. The knights were so deep in their plans for the
coming crusade that they marked not his absence.

Heinrich was cordially welcomed by his noble hostess. It was a
glorious evening, the sun was sinking, and Heinrich, who was
longing for solitude, was glad to avail himself of her proposal to
view the grounds of the castle. He hastened into the open air.
From the high rock on which the castle was built he looked down
into a wooded valley, through which ran a stream which turned
several mills on its way; beyond that, ranges on ranges of hills

and woods. In the presence of nature the agitation subsided, the glories of the sunset awoke a thousand fancies, and he longed for a lute to help him to express his feelings, although he neither knew what it was like, nor how to play upon it. He scrambled through a copse, over mossy rocks towards the valley, when he was suddenly arrested by the melodious sound of a human voice, accompanied by harmonious chords. He felt sure it must be a lute, and stood still to listen.

The song ceased, and he heard the sob of a child and a girl's soothing voice. He hurried down the hill, and saw a pale, delicate girl sitting under a spreading oak-tree; a pretty child clung to her in tears; a lute lay at her feet. At the sight of the youth she started with surprise.

"I suppose you heard me singing," she said, in a friendly voice. "Your face seems well known to me; let me think. The sight of you evokes old memories. You are so like one of my brothers, who, after our misfortunes, left us to join a well-known Persian poet. Perhaps he still lives, and sings sadly of his sister's fete. Would that I could recall some of the poems he wrote! He was a noble youth, none excelled him in poetry and music."

The child, a girl about ten or twelve, looked attentively at the new-comer, while she still embraced Zulima. Heinrich's heart was moved with compassion, and he begged the maiden to tell him her story. She seemed willing to do so. He seated himself opposite her, and listened to her sad tale, which was interrupted by many tears. She dwelt principally on her fatherland and her country folk, described their generosity, their susceptibility to the poetry of life, and the wondrous charm of an Eastern existence. She spoke of the picturesque beauty of the Arabian scenery, the oases like happy islands surrounded by sand instead of sea, havens of rest for the weary travellers, who found there cool springs, streams rippling over sparkling stones, through softest lawns, and found a shelter under thick groves animated by the songs of countless birds of gorgeous plumage. Here and there were strange memorials of the past: ruins still gay with pictures of long-vanished scenes, quaint sculpture and mysterious inscriptions, which excited a ceaseless desire to penetrate their hidden message. The presence of these mementos of bygone ages arouse a thousand fresh ideas and reflections, and lend a greater charm to the present; for all around speaks of centuries of toil, care, and forethought. Nature seems bound up in humanity; the present is permeated with the past; so that one enjoys a double life, a gleam of fable and legend softening all the asperities and difficulties of actual existence. Who knows whether there may not be some inexplicable influence haunting the spot, emanating from the former unseen inhabitants; and perhaps this is the cause why dwellers in a newly discovered country feel so intense a longing to return to their old homes." After a pause she continued, "Do not believe what you have been told of the cruelty of my people. Nowhere are prisoners treated more generously; the greatest hospitality was shown to your pilgrims to Jerusalem. Unhappily they did not deserve it. Many were scoundrels of the deepest dye, who repaid the kindness shown them in the most shameful way, and justly deserved their fate. The Christians might have continued their pilgrimages quite unmolested, and without provoking the cruel wars which have separated Europe from the East for ever. What mattered the nominal ownership of the soil? Our princes honoured the grave of your Holy One, whom they looked on as a Holy Prophet. It would have been an easy task to have made this common feeling a stepping-stone to a friendly union."

By this time twilight had faded into night, and the moon rose over the summits of the trees, as they slowly ascended the hill towards the castle. Heinrich was lost in thought, his warlike enthusiasm had evaporated. The world seemed to him a maze of incongruity. The moon, shedding her consoling beams over all, raised his mind above the inequalities of earthly life, which however great when seen close at hand, vanish away when viewed from a higher point. Zulima moved silently beside him, leading the child. Heinrich carried the lute. He sought to cheer his companion, and raise her hopes of one day returning to her much-loved home. He felt inclined to devote himself to her service, and deliver her from her slavery, but he knew not how to accomplish it. His sympathizing words soothed Zulima, and she thanked him in touching accents for this unwonted pity.

The carouse was at its height in the hall. As they entered the castle, Heinrich felt no desire to join the jovial knights, but sought out his mother, who had passed a quiet evening with the lady of the castle. Soon after they retired to rest, but not before Heinrich had told her his strange adventure. They were early astir, and so were the merchants, who had retired be-times from the banquet. The knights were sleeping off their carouse, but the Châtelaine took a friendly leave of the party. Zulima, who had passed a sleepless night, excited by unwonted sympathy, was at her post to wait upon the travellers. As they took leave, she brought her lute and offered it to Heinrich. "It was my brother's," she said; "he gave it me when he went away; it is my only relic of the past. It seemed to please you yesterday, and I offer it as a paltry return for words I shall never forget, and the hope you have again awoke in my heart. I feel we shall meet again, and in happier days."

Heinrich wept, but he refused to take her precious lute. "Give me the golden riband which binds your hair, and on which I see some curious embroidery, unless it is a remembrance of parents or friends."

She handed him the riband. "It is my name, which I embroidered in the letters of my own tongue. Look at it, and remember that it has bound my tresses during a sad and weary time. It has faded, like its owner."

Heinrich's mother handed him a veil, for which he asked, and he offered it to Zulima as a remembrance, then the women kissed and took a tearful leave of each other.

# CHAPTER V

After a few days, they reached a village, at the foot of a mountain range. The country was luxuriant and smiling, in spite of its frowning background of rocks and ravines. The inn was clean, the host obliging, the guest-room was full of country-folk, talking and drinking.

Our travellers soon remarked an old man, dressed in foreign garb, seated at a table. He seemed genial and friendly, and answered all the questions addressed to him. He came from a distant country, and had been busy examining the neighbourhood. He was ready to talk of his profession, and the discoveries of that day. He was a treasure-seeker, the people said; but he himself spoke very modestly about his knowledge and power; still, his remarks bore the stamp of novelty and singularity. He said that he was born in Bohemia. From his earliest youth he had a keen desire to know what was hidden within the mountains, whence water rose, and where gold, silver, and precious stones could be found.

He used to look at the rich ornaments and jewels in the convent church, and long that they had words to tell him whence they came. He had been told they came from far-distant lands; yet he always thought why should not the mountains and rocks near at hand contain similar treasures. It was not for nothing that mountains were so inaccessible and fortified against attack; at times he had himself found sparkling gems in hidden rifts and cracks. His chief delight had been scrambling up heights and into every cave and grotto he could find. At last he met a traveller, who told him he ought to become a miner, and thus satisfy his curiosity. There were mines in Bohemia. If he went down the river he would reach Eula in eight or ten days; he had only to ask, and he would be engaged at once in the mines. He did not require to be told twice, but set off at once. After a fatiguing tramp he reached Eula.

"I cannot tell you," he said, "how delighted I was when I caught sight of heaps of stones half overgrown with bushes, on which were some wooden huts, whose blue smoke rose above the copse. A strange rumbling noise added to my excitement; soon I found myself standing by one of the heaps of stone thrown out from the bowels of the earth. I hurried along the valley, meeting some men dressed in black, holding lamps in their hands. I guessed that they were miners, and, addressing them, told my wish. They were kind and friendly, and desired me to go on to the smelting hut and to ask for the head man; he would tell me if he would take me or not. They thought I should have no difficulty, and taught me their usual greeting, 'Glück auf' (Good luck to you), with which to address the head man. I pursued my way in high glee, repeating the expressive formula.

"At last I found a reverend old man, who received me kindly, and who promised, when I had told my story, to give me the work I so longed for.

"He seemed pleased that I was so attracted by his strange, mysterious craft, and led me to his own house to rest. I could scarcely bear to wait a moment before being introduced into the new life.

"That evening he brought me a mining suit, and explained the use of the tools I should have to use.

"In the evening the miners came to him, and I listened eagerly to their talk, much of which was quite incomprehensible to me. The little which I gleaned increased my curiosity, and haunted me in my dreams. I awoke very early, and found the miners all assembled. An adjacent hut was simply arranged as a chapel, a monk appeared and said a mass, then poured out a fervent prayer, invoking God's protection on the miners in their perilous calling, and entreating that they might be safe from the wiles of evil spirits. I had never prayed with deeper devotion, nor understood more clearly the hidden significance of the mass. My future comrades seemed like heroes going in quest of danger, and also as possessors of a much-envied happiness in learning nature's hidden mysteries, and, communing in solitude with the rocks, her mighty sons. The head man gave me after service a lamp, a small wooden crucifix, and accompanied me to one of the shafts. He taught me how to go down, and told me what precautions to take, as he slid down the yawning chasm astride on a round beam, holding in one hand a burning lamp, and in the other a knotted rope, which slipped through a pole alongside us. We soon reached a great depth. I felt it a solemn moment when my guide preceded me with his light, shining like a star in the gloom, to introduce me to nature's hidden treasure-house.

"We soon reached a labyrinth of passages, and my guide was unwearied in answering my questions, and instructing me in his trade. The old man was delighted with my enthusiasm, and prophesied that I should be a capital miner. How can I describe my delight when on the sixteenth of March, forty-five years ago, I saw for the first time the king of metals lying in thin streaks in the crevice of a rock! I thought it shone joyfully on its deliverer, who came to set it free from its dark hiding-place, to bring it out to the light of day, where it might assume its rightful, position in the crowns of kings, the reliquaries & saints, or become the honoured medium of commerce, ruling the world by its power.

"From that moment I remained at Eula, passing through every gradation of work, until I reached the post of gem-cutter."

Here the old man stopped to rest and drink with his companions, who heartily shouted "Glück auf". While he rested, they talked of the strange life of the miners, and related many legends, which made the treasure-hunter laugh.

"You must have had strange experiences, and seen marvellous things," said Heinrich. "Did you ever repent of the mode of life you had adopted? Pray tell us your next adventures, and the object you have now in view. It seems to me you have seen more of the world and know far more than a mere miner."

"I love to speak of the past," said the old man; "it recalls vividly the goodness and mercy which have led me on my way. Fate has granted me a merry, happy life. I have ever lain down at night in rest and peace. I have prospered in all my undertakings. Our Father in heaven has preserved me from evil, and given me the respect of all in my old age. Next to Him, I owe everything to my old master at the mine, who has long since been gathered to his fathers, but whom I can never think of without tears. He was a man of the olden days, a man after God's heart. He was gifted with keen penetration, yet he was ever humble and childlike. The great success of the mines was all owing to him; he produced enormous treasures for the Dukes of Bohemia. The neighbourhood became populous and flourishing, and riches and prosperity increased. The miners looked on him as a father. As long as Eula stands, his name will be honoured. He was a Lusatian, called Werner. When I came to him his only daughter was a child. Every day he seemed more pleased with my diligence, my faithfulness, and my devotion to him. He gave me his name, and called me his son. The little girl was a bright, merry child, with a white skin as even as her temper. When I played and joked with her, admiring her eyes, which were as blue as the heavens, and shone like crystal, Werner would say, 'Be a good miner, and I will not refuse her to you;' and he kept his word.

"The day when I became gem-cutter he laid our hands together, and gave us his blessing. That very morning I discovered a rich vein of gold. The Duke sent me his likeness on a golden coin, hanging to a heavy gold chain, and promised that I should succeed Werner in his office. How proud I was to wear it on my marriage day, and see all eyes fastened on it.

Our old father lived many years, and rejoiced over his

grandchildren. Then he tranquilly abandoned the shafts in which his life had passed, left the dark earth where he had laboured, and went to his rest, to await the great day of reward.

"Sir," said the old man, turning to Heinrich, and wiping away a tear, "mining must be under the blessing of God. There is no craft which makes men nobler and happier, which awakens greater faith in heavenly wisdom and forethought, or in which men preserve greater innocence of heart-life. The miner is born poor, and dies poor. It is enough for him that he knows the hiding-places of the metallic powers, and can bring them forth to light; but their brilliancy does not raise thoughts of covetousness in his pure heart. Untouched by this dangerous madness, he delights more in their marvellous formations, the strangeness of their origin, and the nooks in which they are hidden, than in their possession. As soon as they become articles of trade, they have lost any attraction in his eyes: he would rather seek for them amidst a thousand dangers in the depths of the earth than win them above ground by art and trickery. Danger keeps his spirit quick, his mind alert; he enjoys his poor dole with a thankful heart, and rises each day with renewed love of life out of the dark pit where he follows his craft.

"He, and he only, appreciates the charm of light and rest, the beneficent influence of fresh air, and a wide view; to him meat and drink are refreshing and quickening, even as the body of the Lord; and with what loving cordiality does he not meet his comrades, and embrace his wife and children, grateful for the beautiful gift of speech?

"His business cuts him off from the usual life of man, and prevents his sinking into dull indifference as to the deep supernatural tie which binds man to heaven. He keeps his native simplicity, and sees in all around its inherent beauty and marvel. Nature abhors selfishness. Hence, her treasures, meant for all, turn to virulent poison when grasped for the selfish use of one man; they drive away his rest, and draw him into a circle of ruinous pleasures, bringing sorrow and wild passions in their train. They thus dig the grave of their possessor, who falls down a fearful precipice, leaving them to circulate freely from hand to hand, and thus satisfy their socialistic craving.

"How patiently does the miner work on in the deep abyss, away from the tumult of the world, desiring only knowledge, and loving union and peace. In his loneliness he thinks lovingly of his family and his friends, and feels the claims of humanity, and the interdependence of all mankind. His calling teaches him endless patience, nor permits his mind wandering in idle thought. He has to conquer a hard, resisting mass, to overcome its power by obstinate diligence and ceaseless attention. How rich is the harvest which he wins. In these obscure depths there grows the deepest faith in his heavenly Father, whose hand guides and preserves him in countless dangers. How often have I sat down, and, by the light of my lamp, contemplated my crucifix with deepest devotion: the true meaning of that holy symbol became clearer to my mind, and my soul seemed for a time set free from the husk of mortality.

"He must have been a godlike man who first taught the noble craft of mining, and traced in the rocks so striking an image of life. Here the vein is high and wide, but poor; there the vein is squeezed in by rocks full of the richest metals; again it yields little but dross, until a friendly lead runs into it, and raises its value a hundredfold. Often it breaks down altogether, but the patient miner goes on undismayed, and his zeal is rewarded by striking on it again in increased richness and facility of working. He is often deceived, and strays from the right direction; but finding out his mistakes, breaks down the intervening obstacles till he reaches the true golden strata. Thus the miner is exposed to all the caprices of fortune, though he retains the belief that only through diligence and perseverance can he overcome them, and obtain the bravely guarded treasure."

"I suppose," said Heinrich, "you must have many songs peculiar to the miner's craft. Music must be a welcome companion of so solitary a life."

"That is true," responded the old man; "song and the zither are part of a miner's life. No class of men are more susceptible to melody. The miner loves music and dancing; they refresh his soul like happy prayers, and the remembrance sweetens many an hour of toil and solitude. If you like, I will sing one which was in every miner's mouth in my days: –

"He of Earth the true lord is
   Who knows her hidden treasure;
The secrets of the rocks are his,
   In them he finds his pleasure.

"To him she tells her story
   Of mighty cycles past,
Recalls the ages hoary
   In forms that ever last.

"The gold he finds is for his king.
   He takes none for himself,
Content to toil, and laugh, and sing,
   And scorn base love of self.

"Men in the plains may rave and fight
   For what is little worth;
He on his hill loves only right.
   And is true king of Earth."

Heinrich begged for more songs, and wrote them down in remembrance of the pleasant meeting.

Soon after, the old man left the room, and the merchants and the other guests began to discuss what he had told them, and form theories as to his present plans.

"Depend upon it," said one, "he has not come here for nothing. All the morning he has been climbing about the hills; let us ask him what he found."

"We should do well," said another, "to ask him to find a spring near the village – we have to go far to fetch water."

"I," said a third, "will ask him to take one of my sons with him; the lad is always bringing home pockets full of stones. I am sure it would just suit him to be a miner."

The merchants, for their part, thought that through him they might find a fresh opening for trade in Bohemia, and might procure metals at a cheap rate.

Soon the old miner returned, and they all sought to make the best use of the opportunity.

"How hot and oppressive this room is," said he. "Outside there is a glorious moonlight; and I feel inclined for a walk. This morning I discovered a remarkable cavern near here. Will some of you come with me, and take torches that we may explore it?"

The villagers knew of the cavern, but had never ventured in. They believed that it was inhabited by dragons and wild beasts; others said it was haunted, and vowed they had seen strange forms go in and out, and heard weird music in the dead of night issuing from it

The old miner laughingly assured them that they would be quite safe under his guidance; the dragons would be afraid of him, and a singing ghost must be a good spirit. Curiosity led some to accept his offer. Heinrich, with some difficulty, obtained his mother's permission to join the party, and the merchants took the same determination. Pitch-pine was collected for torches, others carried ropes, ladders, poles, and all sorts of weapons. The old miner, Heinrich, and the merchants went first. The peasant fetched his stone-loving boy, who was delighted to show the way, and carry a torch. The moon rose gloriously over the hills, giving a dream-like appearance to the landscape. Heinrich was bewitched with the beauty around him; he felt as if nature were about to reveal her treasures to him. The words of the old miner had opened up fresh trains of thought: his life hitherto seemed narrow and dark, now his imagination wandered away to the far-distant past and its mysteries; then pictured the glorious future, the fellowship with the angels above, whose silvery tones seemed to float in the air. He realized for the first time the bond which united him to nature, all she had taught and would yet make known to him. The merchant's story of the youth who studied nature's ways rose to his mind, and mingled with a thousand remembrances of his life. At last they reached the grotto. The entrance was low. The old man, taking a torch, was the first to enter. The timid peasants came last, shouldering their poles and axes. Heinrich and the merchants kept close to the old miner, and the peasant boy went merrily beside them. The narrow entrance led to a large, high-vaulted cavern, which was so vast that their torches were insufficient to reveal all its beauties; but they could perceive further openings in the rocks. The ground was covered with soft sand, the walls and roof neither rough nor irregular; but what attracted their attention most was the immense quantity of bones and teeth lying on the ground. Many were in perfect preservation, others in the wall seemed to be fossils. They were all very large and strong. The old miner was delighted with these relics of the past; but the peasants were much alarmed, for they felt sure they were the proof that wild beasts lived in the cavern. It was in vain that the miner told them they were bones of animals such as they had never seen, then asked them if they had ever missed any of their flocks and herds. Reason and argument failed to convince them, and they judged it wiser to retreat to the entrance of the cave, and await the return of those who were inclined to tempt their fate. Heinrich, the merchants, and the boy alone remained with the old man, and provided themselves with ropes and ladders. They soon reached a second cavern, carefully marking the passage by which they had come with a collection of bones. This cavern was like the last, and as rich in animal remains. Heinrich felt as if wandering through the courts of a secret palace. Heaven and earth were far away; he had entered a new region of marvels. A strange, new life was close by him. What fiery nature had given birth to these monstrous beings whose skeletons lay strewn around? He imagined himself surrounded by the living forms of these huge pre-Adamite monsters, as in those far-off ages, when angelic beings were also visible in the air, occupied with man's future dwelling-place. Were these gigantic bones a natural deposit after the extinction of life, or had these mammoths taken refuge in the clefts of the rock to escape some tremendous convulsion of nature?

All at once the old miner called his companions, and pointed to recent traces of human footsteps. There were but few, which made it improbable that they were on the track of a band of robbers; so they determined to push on. As they were on the point of doing so, they were arrested by a sound rising from beneath, soft and musical. They listened, and heard the following words: –

"Naught fear I in these darksome shades –
I have a love that never fades.
My soul is nigh to Heaven's gate –
No mortal has a happier fate.
For though I've passed long, weary years,
The hope of Heaven has checked my fears;
And when the joyful call is given,
My grateful soul will rise to Heaven."

So sweet were the tones that they longed to discover the singer.

After searching for some time, they discovered a passage in a comer of the wall, which seemed to lead downwards. In a short time they perceived a glimmer of light, which grew brighter and brighter as they proceeded. At last they entered a large, vaulted grotto, and saw a man at one end, reading, by the light of a lamp, out of a large book which rested on a slab of rock.

When he saw them, he rose and came towards them. It was difficult to say whether he were old or young, for his face bore no signs of age, though his locks were silvery. His countenance was inexpressibly attractive and cheerful, like that of some one looking from a mountain on a scene of perpetual spring. He was wrapped in a mantle, which increased the effect of his height, and wore sandals on his feet.

He did not seem in the least surprised at the sight of such unexpected visitors.

"I am much pleased to see you," he said. "In all the years I have lived here, I have never before had a visitor. It seems to me people are waking up, and finding out more of the wonderful abode which has been given us."

"We did not expect to meet so friendly a host," replied the old miner; "we heard many tales of wild beasts and ghosts. Forgive us, if, in our curiosity, we have disturbed you in your deep meditations."

"What is more attractive than the sight of genial, happy, human faces? Do not think that I am a misanthrope because you find me living in this solitude. I have not fled from the world. I have only sought a place of rest where I could meditate undisturbed."

"Have you never repented of that resolution? and are there not moments when you long for a human voice?"

"Not now. In my early youth my enthusiasm led me to become a hermit. My youthful imagination brooded over dark presentiments. I thought that I could find inexhaustible treasures in myself. But I soon found out that a young life cannot brook loneliness. One must have the experiences of a lifetime to think over. Youth only acquires independence by intercourse with fellow-beings."

"I can believe," responded the old miner, "that there are certain natures inclined to solitude; and perhaps the experiences of increasing age lead one to withdraw from society. There is both instruction and amusement to be gained in social intercourse. Common objects and interests draw men together, quite apart from children and old people. The former are excluded by reason of their ignorance and powerlessness, the latter because their objects are attained, their hopes fulfilled. They can no longer join in the circles of everyday life. They draw apart, to prepare for a higher community. But you seem to have had special motives in thus cutting yourself adrift from men, and resigning all the interests and conveniences of life. At times surely your spirits must flag, and dreariness steal over you?"

"That is true. But I live so methodically that I can overcome it. Occupation and exercise are absolutely necessary for health. Every day I walk for miles, and enjoy the air and light. At other times I occupy myself with basket-weaving and carving, which I exchange in the neighbourhood for provisions. I brought many books here, and time slips rapidly away. I have a few acquaintances who know where I live, and who keep me informed of all that goes on in the world. When I die they will bury me, and inherit my books."

He then led them nearer to his seat, which was close to the wall of the cavern. Many books were lying on the ground, and a zither; on the wall hung a complete suit of armour, richly inlaid. The table was made of great stone slabs, placed together like a chest. On the uppermost slab lay two carved stone figures, life-size, holding between them a wreath of lilies and roses. Round the sides ran this inscription, "Here Friedrich and Maria von Hohenzollern returned to their fatherland."

The hermit then asked his guests many questions about their homes, and what had brought them to the cavern. He was very open and communicative, and showed a great knowledge of the world.

"I see," said the old miner, "you have been a soldier. That armour betrays you."

"It is true. The changes and dangers in a soldier's life powerfully attracted me, and made me throw up my first attempt at a hermit's life. Perhaps the turmoil and strange events which I passed through really increased my love for solitude. My countless adventures are pleasant company for me; all the more so that I now look back on them in a widely different spirit to that which then ruled me. I see now more clearly the sequence of events and their meaning. One can judge much more clearly in calm repose than in the tumult of action; and it is only when one contemplates a long sequence of events in the history of man, that one perceives how one circumstance evolves another, linked by the chain of the past and the future. The key of history is knowledge of the past. We grope among incomprehensible and incomplete problems, and rejoice when we stumble on any teaching which makes our own short span more clear to us. All thoughtful study of the destiny of life is fraught with deep enjoyment, and enables us more than anything else to rise above the evils around us.

"Young people read history only from curiosity, like an interesting fairy tale; to old age history is a divine, consoling friend, who, by her wise remarks, prepares the mind for a higher and nobler-sphere. The church is the home of History, the churchyard her flower-garden. Only old and God-fearing people, whose own history draws to a close, should write of the past. There would be nothing dreary or sad in their views; on the contrary, they would be illumined from on high, and the Holy Spirit would move on the strangely agitated waters."

"Your remarks are very true," said the old miner; "doubtless one should use more diligence in transmitting a true picture of one's time to posterity, so as to help future generations. We trouble ourselves about a thousand things, but neglect the nearest and most important – our own fate, and that of those connected with us; never seeing the well-combined plan of Providence, and allowing the most striking incidents to be effaced by trifles. Wise descendants would look upon a truthful account of the life of even an insignificant man as a priceless heirloom, as in it would be reflected the tone of his age."

"It is sad," said the Count of Hohenzollern, "that the few who have described the deeds and occurrences of their own times have done so without due consideration, and that their remarks are so incomplete and vague. No one can describe a thing well without a perfect understanding of it. Let a child describe a machine, a peasant, a ship – who can form any idea of the reality? And it is the same with most historians, who may be full of gossip and long-winded, but who forget what is the most essential, that which is alone worthy of the name of history, and which links cause and effect in one harmonious whole. When I consider the matter, it seems to me that an historian ought to be a poet, for only a poet knows the art of combination. I have been delighted with their tender sympathy with the mysterious influences of life. There is more truth in their fairy tales and fables than in learned chronicles. Even if their events and characters are creatures of the imagination, the spirit in which they are described is true and natural. Whether the persons whose fate foreshadows ours ever lived or not is of no importance, as regards the instruction and enjoyment we derive from them. We long for great, simple types of life; and when a wish is granted, we do not care whether the form in which they are presented is genuine."

"I also have always loved poets," said the old man, "they have made life clearer and more comprehensible to me. They are connected with the spirits of light, who permeate nature, casting a daintily coloured veil over all. Songs have ever found a ready response in my heart, stirring me up to fresh exertions, making my mind alert and happy."

"Were you so happy as to have any poets in your neighbour-hood?" asked the hermit.

"Occasionally, but they were all fond of travelling, and never stayed long. But I have met many in my wanderings through Illyria, Saxony, and Sweden, of whom I keep a grateful memory."

"If you have roamed so far, you must have seen many strange things."

"Our science requires an extended acquaintance with the earth; a miner is driven on by an inner fire. One hill sends him to another. He is never weary of investigating; all his life he is learning. Our craft is very ancient and widespread. It has come from the East, like our race. Everywhere it has to struggle with difficulties, but man's necessities have ever stimulated his invention, so every difficulty conquered increases the miner's resources, and helps him to enrich his country."

"You are inverted astronomers," replied the hermit, "they consider the formation of the heavens; you look downwards and investigate the structure of the earth. They study the attractions and influences of the stars: you discover the uses and capabilities of the metals and rocks, and the varied strata. To the one, the heaven speaks of the future; while the other evokes memories of past ages from below the earth."

"This connection is not meaningless," said the miner. "Those glittering prophets played a great part in the formation of this globe. Perhaps in time we may understand the influence of their actions, and from the results comprehend their nature. Perhaps the great mountain chains are traces of their passage. Some rose proudly higher and higher, as if to join the stars, and as a punishment lost the green vesture of lowlier regions. In compensation they have become weather prophets to the valleys, which they sometimes protect, sometimes overwhelm with storms."

"Since I have dwelt in this cavern," continued the hermit, "I have reflected more on the early ages. It is strange how attractive the subject is; it makes one understand a miner's devotion to his craft. When I see the heaps of strange old bones collected here, I think of the primitive ages when the enormous antediluvian animals swarmed in these caverns, driven here, perhaps, by some sudden panic. Then I picture the earth covered with water. How quiet and peaceful is nature now to what she was then! The most terrible storm or earthquake now is but a faint echo of the former throes and convulsions which shook the earth. Probably in those days men and plants, as well as animals, were on a rougher, larger scale, and the giants may have been no fancied legend."

"It is indeed cheering," said the miner, "to see how calm and peaceful nature is now. There seems to be everywhere a greater balance of power and more peaceful cohesion. We can look forward to still better days. Some of the old leaven may still give rise to mighty convulsions. Nature seems striving to attain greater harmony, and these convulsions will pass over, and only hasten the general good. It may be that nature is no longer so productive as of yore; no new metals, precious stones, mountains, and hills are produced; men and animals are smaller; but if her productive power has diminished, her tendency is gentler, softer, more ennobling, her fancy richer and more varied, her hand lighter and more artistic.

"There is no need to increase her treasure, it will suffice for ages and ages. I have roamed through but a small portion of the world, and yet I have seen the mighty wealth amassed for coming generations. What riches are hidden in the mountains of the North, all through my fatherland, and in the rocks of the Tyrol, Austria, and Bavaria! I would have been a rich man had I carried off all I could have picked up. In many places I thought I was in an enchanted garden. I was surrounded by costly metals formed in the most artistic shapes. Transparent ruby fruit hung on the daintily moulded branches of silver trees, which rose from a crystal floor of surpassing loveliness. One could hardly trust one's eyes in these regions of marvel, and one never wearied going through such magic scenes. In my present journey I have seen many remarkable things, and no doubt other lands offer as rare sights."

"Yes," said the hermit, "there is no doubt of that. Think of the treasures of the East India, Africa, and Spain were known to the Ancients by their riches. As a soldier, I had but little time to think of the hills and their hidden treasures; yet I often cast a curious eye on the shining veins of metal which spoke of unseen beauty. Little did I then think that I should end my life in the heart of a mountain. When the war ended I returned home to pass the tranquil Autumn of my life. My Marie had given me two children in the East. The fatigues of travel and the rougher climate of the West faded their bloom; I lost them a few days after we landed in Europe. Sadly I took my wife to my home, but sorrow had cut the thread of her life, and on a journey in which she went with me as usual, she died in my arms. Our pilgrimage ended near here. My determination was quickly taken. A divine inspiration came to me; I buried her here with my own hands; and since that day all sorrow has been banished by a divine influence. I have had this tomb erected to her. God grant you all as happy an old age and as peaceful a conscience as mine."

Heinrich and the merchants had listened with deep attention. The hermit's words fell like good seed in the young man's mind, and woke him out of the narrow circle in which he had lived. The past years seemed far behind him, and he fancied he had never felt or thought otherwise than he did at that moment.

The hermit then showed them his books. They were old histories and poems. Heinrich turned over the beautifully illuminated pages. The short lines of the poetry, the headings, and the dainty pictures all aroused his curiosity. The hermit observed his interest, and explained the various pictures. There were scenes of all kinds: camps, funerals, marriages, shipwrecks, huts, and palaces; kings, heroes, priests, old and young people in strange costumes, and wild beasts from distant lands. Heinrich was never weary looking at them, and would have liked nothing better than to stay in the cavern and learn all the hermit could teach him.

The old miner asked if there were more caverns at hand. The hermit assured him there were, and offered to show them to him. As he saw Heinrich's devotion to the books, it was settled that he should stay where he was while the others examined the subterranean marvels.

Heinrich thanked him heartily for the permission, and turned over the leaves with ever-increasing delight. At last he opened a book written in a strange tongue, something like Latin and Italian. The book charmed him, and he grieved that he could not read it. It had no title, but some pictures which struck him dumb with amazement, he thought he was in a dream when he recognized himself; the longer he looked the more strange it seemed. There he was in the cavern beside the hermit and the old miner; other pictures represented his parents, the Landgraf and Landgrävin of Thuringia, his tutor the Court Chaplain, and many of his friends; but their costumes were those of another age. A number of figures seemed familiar to him, though he knew not their names. Towards the end he seemed to have grown nobler and taller. He held a guitar in his arms; the Landgrävin gave him a cross. Again he was on board ship, at Court, kissing a tall lovely maiden, surrounded by wild-looking men, Saracens and Moors.

The last pictures were dark and incomprehensible, and the end was wanting. Heinrich longed to possess the wondrous volume; he looked at it again and again, and started with surprise at the return of the explorers.

A strange timidity crept over him, and he scarcely ventured to ask the hermit in what language it was written. "In the Provencal tongue," he replied. "It is long since I read it. I do not remember the contents. As far as I can recall, it is a romance about a poet and his wanderings. The end, you see, is wanting. I brought it from Jerusalem, in remembrance of a friend to whom it had belonged."

They took leave. Heinrich was moved to tears. The experiences in the cavern had been so strange and he had felt so drawn towards the hermit

They all embraced each other tenderly, and Heinrich perceived that the hermit looked at him with kind but piercing glances. His last words were peculiar, and seemed to show that he knew of Heinrich's discovery in the book. He accompanied them to the entrance, after begging them and the peasant boy not to betray his abode to the peasants. This they all promised. As they went, they begged him to pray for them.

"How long will it be," said he, "before we meet again, and, perhaps, smile at our talk to-day? A heavenly light will then surround us, and we shall rejoice that we met in these valleys of trial, and exchanged our thoughts in genial intercourse. Thoughts are the angels which guide us here below. If your eye is fixed on your home above, you cannot lose the way."

They departed with a feeling of awe, and soon joined their frightened companions, who told them country tales all the way back to the village, where they were joyfully welcomed by Heinrich's mother, who had been in great anxiety as to their prolonged absence.

# CHAPTER VI

Men of action can never begin too soon to see and act for themselves. They require to pass through many varied circumstances and difficulties to acquire firmness, so that in the greatest pressure of life they may yet hold to their own purpose, and carry it to completion. They must not yield to the charm of meditation. Their spirit must be ceaselessly directed outwards, and be the diligent, active servant of reason. They are heroes, who must lead events and solve life's difficulties. Their influence turns all things into history. Their life is an unbroken chain of remarkable, dazzling, involved, and strange occurrences.

How different is the existence of those quiet, unknown beings, whose world is feeling, whose activity is meditation, and whose life is the counterpart of their character. No restlessness drives them into action. Silent possession satisfies them. The everchanging scenes around have no attraction for them, save as a subject of thought in their leisure hours. They are the soul of the world, even as the men of action are the members.

Great and varied experiences would only disturb them. A simple life is their best fate, and they only know the varied trials and scenes of life through books and conversation. Occasionally events drag them into the whirl of existence, as if to teach them the character and behaviour of men of action. On the other hand, their sensitive natures make fresh and surprising discoveries in the most simple and commonplace things, as well as in themselves.

These are poets, men of influence who wander amongst us, recalling mankind to their old adoration of the stars, spring, love, happiness, health, and merriment. They seem already possessed of heavenly calm. No earthly desires agitate their breasts. They breathe the odours of earth's sweetest fruits without devouring them. They are welcome guests, whose light footsteps call out the hidden angel in every heart. Like a good king, the poet wakes all around to happiness. He alone has a right to the name of wise. He arouses heroism in youthful breasts, though heroic deeds have never aroused the spirit of poetry. Heinrich was a born poet. Varied events united to educate him. As yet, nothing had stirred the depths of his being. Everything which he saw and heard seemed the drawing back of bolts, and opening of fresh windows for his soul. He saw the world in its strange complexity before him. As yet, it was silent and had not spoken to his heart. But a poet was at hand, and a lovely maiden, at the sound of whose lute his heart would awake.

The journey was over. It was evening when our travellers, happy and unwearied, reached the world-famed town of Augsburg, and drove through its busy streets to old Schwaning's handsome house.

Heinrich was delighted with everything; the stir of busy folks, and the high stone houses; and looked forward with pleasure to his visit. His mother was happy in the prospect of resting after her fatiguing journey, and meeting her father and many old friends, introducing her Heinrich to them, and living for a time free from all domestic cares. The merchants looked forward to merry-makings and profitable business. Old Schwaning's house was brilliantly lighted up, and the sound of merry music struck their ears as they drove up.

"Your grandfather is having a feast," said the merchants. "We are in luck. How surprised he will be at his unexpected guests. Now the real festivities will begin."

Heinrich felt shy; his mother anxious about her dress. They got out, and entered the stately mansion, leaving the merchants with the horses. The lower floor was deserted. They ascended the handsome winding stair. Some servants ran forward, whom they asked to call old Schwaning, as some strangers wished to see him. The servants made difficulties – the travellers did not look like expected guests – but at last they went to their master. Old Schwaning came. At first he did not know them, and asked them their names and their business. Heinrich's mother wept, and, throwing her arms round his neck, cried, "Do you not know your own daughter? Here is your grandson."

The old father was much moved. He pressed her to his heart. Heinrich fell on one knee and kissed his hand; but his grandfather quickly raised him up and embraced him.

"Quick! come in; I have only friends and old acquaintances with me. They will all welcome you heartily."

Heinrich's mother hesitated; but her father gave her no time to answer, but led her into the brilliantly lighted hall.

"Here are my daughter and my grandson from Eisenach," called out Schwaning to the merry groups of richly clad guests.

All eyes turned to the door, all hastened forward, the music stopped, and the dusty, travel-stained travellers stood confused and dazzled amid the brilliant throng.

A thousand kind welcomes passed from mouth to mouth. Old friends pressed round the mother. There were innumerable questions. Each one wished to be the first recognized and greeted.

While the elders were absorbed in the mother, the younger people present looked at the youth, whose eyes were cast down, as if unwilling to meet the gaze of so many strangers. Schwaning had introduced him to them, and asked about his father and the incidents of the journey.

Heinrich's mother now told her father about the merchants, who were still on horseback at the door. A message was sent at once, inviting them to enter. Their horses were taken to the stables, and the merchants appeared.

Schwaning thanked them heartily for their friendly escort to his daughter. They knew many of the guests, who greeted them. Heinrich's mother wished to change her dress, so Schwaning took her and Heinrich to their rooms.

Heinrich's quick eyes had perceived among the guests a man whose face he had seen in the hermit's book always near his own picture.

His noble bearing at once attracted attention. His face was grave but cheerful; his broad forehead, black penetrating eyes, and a certain humorous smile round the mouth, made it most attractive. He was tall and strongly built, every motion calm and expressive; when he stood still it seemed almost as though he were a statue. Heinrich asked his grandfather who he was.

"I am glad that you remarked him; he is my dearest friend, Klingsohr, the poet. You may be prouder of his acquaintance and friendship than of the Emperor's. But beware of your heart, for he has a lovely daughter, who may attract you more. I should not be surprised if you had already observed her."

Heinrich blushed. "There were so many present, grandfather, and I had eyes only for your friend."

"It is easy to see that you come from the North", said Schwaning. "We will thaw you here. You shall learn to admire lovely eyes."

When they returned to the hall, supper was being set. Schwaning led Heinrich up to the poet, and told him that his grandson had remarked him at once, and wished to know him.

Heinrich felt timid at first, but Klingsohr's voice was so sympathetic, his conversation so friendly, that he soon felt quite at his ease. In a short time Schwaning returned with the pretty Matilda.

"Be kind to my grandson, and forgive him for noticing your father first. Your brilliant eyes will awaken him; spring comes late in the North."

Heinrich and Matilda blushed, and looked at one another with surprise. She asked him in a low voice if he liked dancing. Just then the musicians struck up a merry strain; Heinrich offered her his hand, and led her off to join the dancers.

Schwaning and Klingsohr watched them, and Heinrich's mother and the merchants admired the graceful pair. Numerous old friends surrounded Heinrich's mother and congratulated her on her handsome son.

Klingsohr said to Schwaning, "He has an attractive face, an investigating, clear-sighted mind, and his voice comes straight from the heart."

"I hope," replied Schwaning, "that he will be your pupil. I think he is a born poet, and has something of your spirit. He is less passionate and determined than his father, who was full of promise in his youth, and ought to have been more than a diligent and clever artist.

Heinrich wished the dance would never end. He looked admiringly at his partner. Eternal youth shone in her large brown eyes; her nose and brow were daintily fashioned; her face like a lily raised to greet the dawn; the blue veins of her delicate white neck made fascinating curves on her tender cheeks; her voice was like a distant echo, and her soft curly brown hair waved round her slight form. The dance ended, and the elders seated themselves at supper at one table, leaving the young folks to sup by themselves.

Heinrich sat by Matilda; a young relation at her left, and Klingsohr opposite. Veronica was as talkative as Matilda was silent; but Heinrich had no ears for her chatter. Klingsohr asked him about the curious riband which was fastened to his coat. Heinrich, in a few touching sentences, told the sad story of the daughter of the East. Matilda wept, and Heinrich could scarcely repress his emotion.

Conversation became general. Matilda told him of Hungary, which her father often visited, and about the life at Augsburg. All were merry. Music stimulated their fancy. Baskets of lovely flowers adorned the table, exhaling sweetest perfume, and wine circulated freely, shutting out the world as with a fairy web.

Heinrich saw for the first time what a feast could be. A thousand merry sprites seemed hovering over the scene, entering into the joys of the mortals whose fancies and imaginations they quickened and enlivened.

Enjoyment rose before him like a golden tree laden with dazzling fruit. Evil hid itself from sight, and it seemed impossible that human love of pleasure could lead to sad knowledge of life, and turn to war and strife. He felt the effect of the rich wine and the costly viands. The goblet seemed sparkling with the glory of earthly enjoyment.

Just then some maidens brought a garland of flowers to old Schwaning, who kissed them, put it on, and told them to fetch one for the poet. He then made a sign for the music, and sang with a loud voice a merry song which made the old folks laugh and the maidens blush.

A wreath was brought and presented to Klingsohr with many sportive jests.

"We must beg of you to sing more respectfully about maidens."

"Certainly, I shall not betray your secrets. Tell me, what will you have?"

"Anything, except a love-song; a drinking-song, if you like."

Klingsohr rose and sang, with a deep, melodious voice, –

"Among green hills the god was born
　　Who brings to us such pleasure,
The sun poured on him that bright morn,
　　Light without stint or measure.

"In Spring he rises gay and bright,
　　And swells the sap in every vine;
And when the harvest fields are white,
　　Our Bacchus reigns the god of wine,

"Men lay him in a narrow bed,
　　A dark sepulchral lair;
But there he dreams of feasts and war,
　　Builds castles in the air.

"Let none approach the silent place
    Where dreams the god of coming power;
For watchmen of an unknown race
    There keep strict watch from hour to hour.

"At last he wakens from his trance,
    He opens wide his sparkling eyes,
And hurries forth, with steps that dance,
    To greet his faithful votaries.

"His form is robed in crystal sheen,
    A deep-red rose is in his hand;
While round him shouting may be seen
    A merry, laughing, jovial band.

"He sheds his radiance far and near,
    To lighten earthly sorrow;
He gives to love a goblet clear.
    And says, 'Forget the morrow,'

"Of old the poets sang his power.
    His gifts of mirth and gladness;
He in return gave them as dower,
    To kiss away all sadness."

"A fine prophet!" said the girls.

Schwaning laughed heartily, and insisted on his rights.

The girls refused, but in vain.

Veronica, who had been one of the wreath-bearers, came back laughing, and said to Heinrich, "Is it not a fine thing to be a poet?"

Matilda told Heinrich that she played on the guitar.

"How glad I should be to learn from you, I have longed to know how."

"My father taught me; he plays exquisitely," she relied.

"I think," said Heinrich, "I should learn better from you. I long to hear you sing."

"Do not expect too much."

"Oh! I have a right to expect, when your very words are music."

Matilda was silent, and her father began a conversation with him, in which Heinrich expressed himself with such fluency and eloquence that all who heard were surprised. His eyes sparkled, and he turned from time to time to see if Matilda approved. In the animation of the moment he took her hand unobserved, and its silent pressure spoke her approval. Klingsohr drew out all his enthusiasm. Then they all rose from supper. Heinrich and Matilda stood together a little apart. He kissed her hand tenderly; she looked at him with friendly eyes. With a sudden impulse he stooped and kissed her lips; she was surprised, but not angry. "Good Matilda! Dear Heinrich!" was all they said. She pressed his hand and hurried to join her friends. Heinrich stood enraptured. His mother came up to him; he spoke tenderly to her.

"Are you not glad that we came to Augsburg? Does it not please you?"

"Dear mother, I could not have imagined such happiness."

The rest of the evening passed merrily; the old people played cards, the young ones danced. The music was like a sea of joy buoying up all youthful hearts.

Heinrich felt the enchantment of first love and undreamt-of pleasure. Matilda, too, seemed carried away by the entrancing strains, and only faintly hid her confidence and love. Klingsohr had taken a liking to the clever lad, and was pleased with his devotion to his daughter. Nor did it fail to catch the eye of the other maidens, who rejoiced to think that they would thus be rid of a rival.

Night had far advanced ere the party separated. "The first and only feast of my life," said Heinrich, when his weary mother had left him to seek much-needed repose. "It recalls my strange dream. I feel just as I did when I saw the magic blue flower. What is the connection between Matilda and that flower? The face which I saw in that calyx was Matilda's, and I remember also seeing it in the hermit's book. Why was it that there it did not move my heart? She is the very spirit of song, the worthy daughter of her father. She will be the soul of my soul, the guardian of the holy fire of life. What an eternity of faith I consecrate to her. I was only born to honour and serve her, to think of her, and adore her. I am indeed happy to be the one chosen to be her echo, and the mirror of her being. It was no chance occurrence that there was a feast at the end of my journey, the opening scene of a new existence. It could not be otherwise, her very presence makes everything joyful and festive."

He approached the window. The choir of stars still illumined the dark sky, but a gleam of whiteness spoke of the coming dawn.

Heinrich called out enthusiastically, "O you eternal stars, you silent wanderers, I call you to witness my oath! For Matilda I will live, and a changeless faith shall unite our souls. Dawn rises for me – the darkness of night is at an end for ever."

It was late, nearly morning, ere he fell asleep. Wonderful dreams swept through his excited brain. A dark-blue river wound through a verdant plain. A boat floated on the calm waters. Matilda sat in it, rowing, a garland of flowers was on her head, she sang a simple song, and looked at him with sadness in her eyes. His heart felt oppressed, he knew not why. The heavens were cloudless, the river still and smooth, and its calm waters reflected her heavenly countenance.

All at once the boat began to swing round and round. He called out to her with anxious voice. She smiled, and drew in her oars. An indescribable terror seized him; he rushed into the water, but the current carried him away. She signed to him, and seemed to speak. The boat filled with water, still she smiled and looked fearlessly at the whirling stream. All at once the boat disappeared, the waves closed over it, and the river flowed on calmly as before. Consciousness forsook him. He came to himself on dry ground. He must have swum far down the stream: the country around was strange. He could not realize what had happened, but wandered on, lonely and dispirited. He felt wearied to death. A little stream gurgled down a hillside, tinkling like fairy bells. He bathed his parched lips, and hurried on, haunted by the terrible scene through which he had passed. As he went his way, birds and flowers talked to him, and soothed his anguish. Then he heard the simple air Matilda had sung in the boat. Someone touched him. "Dear Heinrich," called a well-known voice. He looked round, and Matilda fell into his arms. "Why did you leave me, dear heart?" said she, panting for breath.

"I could scarcely overtake you."

He pressed her in his arms. "Where is the river?" he asked, with tears in his eyes,

"Do you not see its blue waters above us?"

He looked up – the stream flowed over their heads.

"Where are we, dear Matilda?"

"With our parents."

"Shall we remain together?"

"For ever," she exclaimed, kissing him and whispering a wonderful, mystic word in his ear. He tried to repeat it, when his grandfather called him, and he awoke. He would have given his life to remember that word.

# CHAPTER VII

Klingsohr stood by his bed, and wished him good morning.

"Come and breakfast with me on a hill beyond the town," said he. "This splendid morning will refresh you. Make haste and dress, Matilda is waiting."

Heinrich joyfully accepted the invitation, and in a few minutes was ready. He kissed Klingsohr's hand in his joy.

Matilda looked wonderfully pretty in her simple morning dress, and greeted him kindly. She carried breakfast in a basket on her arm, and held out the other hand to Heinrich. Klingsohr followed them. They soon quitted the bustling streets, and ascended a rising ground, which commanded an extensive view. They seated themselves under some tall trees.

"Much as I love all natural beauty," said Heinrich, "I have never felt in so joyful a mood as to-day. This rich landscape is like a fairy scene, and even the far-off horizon seems near in this clear atmosphere. How changeable is nature, in spite of her apparent sameness. How it alters one's mood, when an angel and a man of intellect share one's enjoyment, instead of having to listen to the murmurs and complaints of a beggar, or a farmer complaining of the weather, and grumbling because there is not enough rain for his crops. Dear master, I owe this pleasure to you – yes, this delight; no other word is strong enough to express my feelings." How he pressed Matilda's hand to his heart, and exchanged a loving glance.

"Nature," said Klingsohr, "is to our feelings what a solid body is to light. It reflects them, breaks them up into varied lines; it lightens our darkness, and enables us in turn to enlighten others. Even the darkest body may be made brilliant by the united action of air, fire, and water."

"I understand you, dear master. Men act as prisms to one another's feelings. Dear Matilda, let me compare you to a sapphire, clear and transparent as the sky, and shedding the softest light. Tell me, dear master, am I right in thinking that the more one loves nature, the less one can talk about it?"

"That depends," answered the poet, "whether you seek enjoyment and sympathy with nature, or exercise your reason in developing and using her gifts. The two objects must be clearly defined. There are many who know but the one, and despise the other. Both, however, can be harmoniously pursued. It is sad that so few strive to attain to a perfect working of all their powers. Too often the one object quenches the other, which gives rise to helpless indolence. When such men rouse themselves to action, they are confused, and stumble awkwardly from one blunder to another. I cannot sufficiently admire your powers of reason, your natural inclination to know causes and effects, and to follow out all natural laws with perseverance and diligence. Nothing is more necessary for the poet than insight into the nature of every craft, knowledge of the means by which ends are attained, and penetration and quickness in choosing that which is most suitable. Intelligence without reflection is dangerous and useless; and the poet who is astonished at what he sees will achieve no marvels."

"Surely the poet requires deep faith in man's power of over-coming destiny?"

"That is true. And how far is this cheerful faith removed from the anxious uncertainty and blind fear of superstition. In the same way the animating warmth of a poet's feelings contrast with the passionate excitement of an unhealthy mind. The one is poor and fugitive, the other firm, clear, and self-sufficing. It is impossible for the young poet to be too cool and collected. True eloquence can alone be melodiously expressed by a calm, attentive mind. If the mind is agitated, the words become confused. Spirit is like light, calm and yet sensitive, it penetrates everywhere, and works unseen and mighty, shedding its influence on everything it touches, and bringing out endless variety. The poet is pure steel, as sensitive as a glass thread, as hard as flint."

"I have often felt," said Heinrich, "that in moments of intense feeling I was less animated than at other times, when free to follow my own business or employments. I seemed under the influence of a constraining power, which seized on all my faculties. How happy I have been when sharing my father's work, rejoicing in being able to help him, and carry out his design. Dexterity has a peculiar attraction, and brings more pure and lasting enjoyment than over-wrought and incomprehensible emotion."

"Do not think that I blame the latter," said the poet; "but it must come unsought. An occasional outburst of emotion is beneficial; but when given way to perpetually, it weakens and wearies the mind. One cannot too soon shake it off, and apply oneself to regular and even toilsome work. It is like the fascinating morning dream, which one must rouse oneself from, under the penalty of passing a weary and spiritless day.

"Poetry," continued Klingsohr, "must be pursued as a severe art. A poet must not run about all day in search of fresh feelings and fancies. That is quite the wrong way. An open mind, the habit of reflection and consideration, the power of translating thought into action, such are the demands our art makes upon us. If you commit yourself to my guidance, not a day must pass without your adding to your knowledge, and attaining fresh insight into art. This town is rich in artists. We have distinguished statesmen, cultivated merchants. Here you can easily become acquainted with all crafts, and all kinds and conditions of men. It will delight me to teach you the practical basis of our art, and read the best writings with you. You may share Matilda's studies, and learn from her how to play the guitar. Every occupation is helpful, and after a busily spent day, you can enter with greater zest into the pleasures of a sociable evening, or appreciate more truly the lovely scenery which surrounds us."

"What a glorious prospect! First you show me the goal, and then offer me your counsel that I may attain it."

Klingsohr embraced him tenderly. Matilda brought breakfast, and Heinrich asked her if she would accept of him as a fellow-student. "I would willingly be your pupil for ever," he whispered, as Klingsohr walked away from them. She bent towards him. He put his arm round her waist, and kissed her rosy lips. Blushingly she released herself, handing him the rose she had worn in her bosom, then stooped to arrange her basket.

Heinrich kissed the rose, fastened it to his breast, and joined Klingsohr, who was admiring the view at a short distance.

"Which way did you approach the town? " asked Klingsohr.

"Over that hill. The road is lost in the distance."

"You must have passed through lovely scenery?"

"The whole route was enchanting."

"Your birthplace is also picturesquresque?"

"The neighbourhood offers great variety, but there is the lack of a fine stream. Rivers are like the eyes of scenery."

"Your account of your journey last night interested me much. The spirit of poetry accompanied you. Your companions were her emissaries. The presence of a poet evokes poetry. The land of poetry, the mysterious East, sent her greetings by the Syrian maiden; the spirit of war stirred your chivalrous feelings; and nature and history were represented in the persons of the old miner and the hermit."

"You do not mention the best of all, dear master – the vision of love. It only depends upon you whether the dream may become a reality."

"What do you mean?" asked Klingsohr, turning to Matilda, who had just joined them. "Are you of a mind to be Heinrich's life-companion?"

Matilda started, and threw herself into her father's arms.

Heinrich trembled with joy.

"Does he desire to be my guide and companion, dear father?"

"Ask him," said Klingsohr, deeply touched.

She looked at Heinrich with gentle, loving eyes.

"My life is in your hands," he said, with tears running down his cheeks.

Klingsohr embraced them both.

"Be faithful until death, my children. Love and faith will make your lives an endless poem."

# CHAPTER VIII

Both Heinrich's grandfather and mother rejoiced over the event of the morning, and looked upon Matilda as a guardian angel for their loved one.

In the afternoon, Klingsohr took him to see his books. Afterwards they talked about poetry.

"I do not know," said Klingsohr, "why nature is commonly termed poetic. There is in nature, as in man, an antagonistic principle of dull indifference and indolence, ever opposed to true poetry. The struggle is a fit subject for a poem. Whole countries and epochs of time seem swayed by this enemy to poetry, whereas other lands and ages seem animated by the true spirit of poetry. Epochs of struggle ought to attract the deepest attention of the historian. They rarely fail in producing a poet. At times the two contending elements seem to exchange identity and weapons; the cruel shafts which her opponent has prepared recoil on her own head, and poetry, overcoming all evil, shines out more attractive and resplendent than of yore."

"War," said Heinrich, "has always seemed to me full of poetry. People fly to arms to defend some wretched possession, and do not see that they are obeying a mighty impulse to overcome evil. Both armies follow an invisible banner."

"War," replied Klingsohr, "is like the rousing of elemental strife. It gives rise to new worlds and new races. But the bitterest of all are religious wars. In them the madness of mankind reaches its apex. Many wars, especially those which rise from national hate, belong to the same class, and are perfect epics. They give birth to the true hero, who is an impersonation of poetry and might. A poet who is at the same time a hero, is a worthy messenger of the gods; but poetry has not as yet portrayed him."

"How so? Is there anything too difficult for poetry?"

"Certainly. Our powers and means of expression are limited. A poet must keep within circumscribed limits, or he gets out of breath and out of keeping. And in the same way, there is a fixed boundary beyond which no man can pass, without losing all force and reality, and sinking into bathos. In youth especially we must guard ourselves from the influence of a hyper-fervid imagination, which leads neophytes to overweening flights of fancy. Experience teaches us to avoid unsymmetrical subjects, and to leave researches into the infinite to philosophy. The riper poet avoids too high a flight, lest he should lose the variety and contrast necessary for the development of his subject. In every poem we can see the chaos out of which it arose. The best poetry is quite close to us, and an every-day subject often lends itself best to treatment. Expression is fettered in poetry, and for that very reason it rises to the dignity of a fine art. Language has its own defined limits: it is only by thought and study that a poet acquires a true knowledge of it. He then appreciates what he can do with his materials, and make no foolish attempt beyond its power. He very rarely puts forth all his strength, in case of wearying the hearer and destroying the due balance of the whole. He is a mere charlatan, and not a poet, who delights in eccentricity. Poets cannot study artists and musicians too much. In these arts it is clearly seen that striking effects must be very rarely adopted, almost everything depends upon skilful treatment. In their turn, those artists must learn from us the inner meaning of everything around. They should grow more poetical, we more musical and artistic, each in the limits of his art. The goal of art is not the subject, but its expression. You will soon see which poems touch you most – certainly those on subjects with which you are familiar. One may say the foundation of poetry is experience. In my youth I loved wild and impossible themes: and what was the result? – miserable windbags, without a spark of genuine poetry. Hence nothing is much more difficult than a fairy tale, and no young poet can succeed in it."

"I should be delighted to hear one of yours," said Heinrich. "I have heard very few, but those charmed me."

"This evening I will do as you wish. I remember one I composed in my youth, of which it bears evident marks. For that very reason, it will be all the more instructive and amusing for you."

"Speech," said Heinrich, "is really a kingdom of signs and harmonies. In the same way that man governs it, he would fain rule the world. Poetry took its origin in man's desire of revealing this inner kingdom to the world, and revelling in the exercise of his hidden faculties."

"Poetry," replied Klingsohr, "ought to have had no special name, nor should the poet be considered as of a separate class. It is but the manifestation of the spirit. Every man, at every moment, is striving to express thought." Just then Matilda entered the room. "Nothing," continued her father, "calls forth the divine gift more than love. Love is dumb, but poetry interprets the feelings of the heart. Love is the highest form of natural poetry. But you know that better than I do."

"You are the father of love," said Heinrich, kissing his hand.

Klingsohr embraced him and left the room.

"Dear Matilda," said Heinrich, after a lover's kiss, "it seems to me a dream that you are mine, but still more wonderful that you have not always been so."

"It seems to me," answered Matilda, "that I have always known you. Do you really love me?"

"I do not know what love is; but this I know, that I feel as if I had just begun to live, and I would gladly die for you. At last I understand what unending life may be."

"My dear Heinrich, how good you are. I am only a poor

insignificant girl; without you I should be nothing. Of what use is a spirit without a heaven to dwell in? and you are the heaven that upholds and supports me. If you are like my father, I shall be the happiest creature on earth. My mother died soon after my birth, and my father has never ceased to lament her. I do not deserve it, but I should like to be happier than he. I hope we may long live together, and that I may daily grow worthier of you."

"Ah! Matilda, death will not separate us. Where you are, I shall be. I cannot comprehend eternity except through my love to you. We are eternal, because we love."

"You cannot think, dear Heinrich, how devoutly I prayed this morning to the Holy Virgin. I was moved to tears, and when I looked at her she seemed to smile. Now I realize what gratitude is."

"Matilda, I adore you. You are the saint through whom I offer my prayers to God, and through whom He has revealed His love. What is religion but the complete union of loving hearts? You are a manifestation of eternal love in its sweetest form."

"Oh, Heinrich, you know the fate of the roses. Will you love pale cheeks and faded lips as well? Will not the traces of old age be the landmarks of departing love?"

"Would, dearest, that you could read my soul! – but you love me, so you believe in me. I cannot imagine that age can make any difference. The soul never grows old. What has attracted me to you is beyond the touch of time. If you could only see the wonderful image in my heart which lightens the whole of life to me, you would never speak of fading charms. Your earthly form is but a shadow of this inward image, the emanation of eternity."

"I understand, dear Heinrich. I feel the same regarding you."

"Matilda, believe me, the spiritual world is nearer to us than we generally think. Already we live in it; it is interwoven with our earthly life."

"Dearest, you make many things clear to me."

"It is from you that this spirit of prophecy has emanated. Everything I have is yours. Your love is the holiest possession of my life; it leads me to the contemplation of all that is noblest and purest. Who knows whether our love may not raise us from earth, and carry us to our heavenly home ere age and death overtake us? is it not a miracle that you are mine, that you love me, and are willing to pass time and eternity with me?"

"I too, feel animated by a holy flame; may it indeed purify our natures, and dissolve all that ties us to earth. Tell me, my Heinrich, have you the same boundless confidence in me that I have in you? I have never felt the same, even in my father, whom I love so deeply."

"Dearest Matilda, it grieves me that I cannot throw my heart open to you. It is the first time in my life that I have desired to share all my feelings with anyone. You must know everything. My whole being seems intermingled with yours. I long to make every sacrifice for your happiness."

"Heinrich, I am sure no lovers have ever loved so much."

"I can quite believe it. There never was another Matilda nor a Heinrich."

"Tell me once again that you are mine for ever; love is never weary of hearing the self-same tale."

"Heinrich, I swear, by the memory of my mother, I am yours for ever."

"Matilda, I swear to be yours for ever, as truly as love has taught us the presence of God."

A tender embrace and untold kisses signed the eternal contract of the loving pair.

# CHAPTER IX

Several guests joined them that evening; the grand-father drank to the health of the betrothed, and asked all present to come to the wedding.

"Why delay?" said he. "Early marriage brings long love. I have always observed that early marriages are the happiest. In later years there is not so much devotion as in youth. A happy youth spent together forms an eternal bond. Memory is the surest foundation of love."

After dinner more friends arrived. Heinrich begged the poet to fulfil his promise.

Klingsohr announced, "I promised Heinrich to-day to relate a fairy tale. If you like to hear it, I am ready."

"That was a capital idea of Heinrich's," said old Schwaning. "It is a long time since you have given us such a treat."

They seated themselves round the blazing fire. Heinrich sat beside Matilda and put his arm round her waist. Klingsohr began his tale.

Night had just fallen. The old hero struck on his shield; the echoes resounded through the deserted streets. Three times he repeated the signal. The high, painted windows in the hall shone in strange brightness, and the figures on them began to move.

The stronger the red light grew, the more animated they became. Light shone on the mighty pillars and massive walls, till they stood out sharp and clear, bathed in an opal hue of many colours. The landscape grew visible, and the neighbouring lake, mountain range and the city, with all its crowds armed with spear and sword. At first, all heads seemed covered with helmets, but these were replaced by crowns which gradually changed into green garlands. A strange noise, like that of an enormous smithy, rose indistinctly from the town. Light increased and spread. The smooth, transparent walls reflected the glow, and one could now see and admire the harmonious symmetry of the building. Dainty vases stood in all the windows, full of snow crystals, which cast luminous rays in all directions.

More beautiful than all was the palace garden, where silver and gold trees glowed with rich fruitage of precious stones. The variety and beauty of their forms and the richness of their colouring contrasted with a mighty frozen *jet d'eau* in the centre.

The old hero paced slowly outside the palace. A voice called to him from within. He gently opened the gate and entered the hall, holding his shield before his eyes.

"Have you seen nothing?" asked the lovely daughter of Arctur, in a complaining tone.

She reclined on silken cushions on a throne, artistically formed of sulphur crystals. Some attendant maidens rubbed her milkwhite feet. As they rubbed, streams of light emanated from the Princess and filled the palace with effulgence. A gentle breeze floated through the hall. The hero held his peace.

"Give me your shield," she said, in a gentle voice.

He approached the throne, and stepped on the soft carpet. She seized his hand, pressed it tenderly to her heart, and touched his shield. His armour rang, his eyes sparkled, and his heart beat fast.

The beautiful Freya seemed gayer, and the light which emanated from her grew more brilliant.

"The King is at hand," cried a gorgeous bird, who was floating over the throne.

The maidens drew at pale-blue drapery over Freya. The hero lowered his shield, and looked up to the cupola, which was reached by two winding stairs at either end of the hall. Music preceded the King, who was soon seen descending, followed by a numerous retinue.

The gorgeous bird spread his wings, fluttered them gently, and sang, like a chorus of a thousand voices –

> "Wake! Princess, wake! from thy long dream,
>   The dawn is nigh, eternity at hand.
> Both land and sea will glow with love's pure beam
>   When comes the stranger from a distant land.
> From hence shall ever banished be the night,
>   When Fable gains again her ancient right"

The King embraced his daughter tenderly. The spirits of the stars gathered round the throne. A countless number of constellations filled Walhalla. The maidens brought in a table and a casket filled with sheets of parchment, on which were inscribed the mystic symbols of the stars. Reverently the King raised them to his lips, then shuffled them together, and, giving some to Freya, retained others in his own hand. The Princess took them up in turn, and laid one on the table; then the King, after deep reflection, chose another, which he laid on it. It seemed as if some unseen power compelled his choice. When the combination was harmonious, his face beamed with joy. All present took the keenest interest, a strange soft music filled the air, while the stars moved in mystic circuits, now quick, now slow. The music changed with the combination produced by the mystic leaves; but though marked by sudden transitions, the theme seemed still the same. The stars, too, formed rapidly in figures, to illustrate the symbols on the table; sometimes collecting in groups, at others in long garlands emitting divine radiance; at one moment gathering round various centres, again forming one symmetrical design. During this time the figures in the lofty windows remained motionless. The bird, however, hovered over the scene.

All at once the King called out joyfully, "All will be right! Eisen, throw your sword into the world, that they may perceive where peace may be found."

The hero drew his mighty sword, pointed it to the sky, then hurled it through the open window, over the town and the frozen lake. It flew like a comet through the air, and splintered on the rocky range, then fell in a thousand sparks.

In those days the beautiful Eros lay in his cradle, and slumbered, while his foster-mother Ginnistan rocked his sister Fable on her knee. She spread her bright shawl over the cradle, that Eros might not be disturbed by the lamp which stood before the scribe. The scribe wrote on, casting angry glances at the children from time to time, and looking gloomily at their nurse, who only laughed to herself.

The children's father came in and out, and looked at them, nodding to Ginnistan. He dictated ceaselessly to the scribe. When his words were written, the leaves were handed to a stately goddess, who leant on one arm on an altar. A dark vase, full of limpid water, stood on the altar. She took the leaves one by one and laid them in the vase. When she drew them out, she looked to see if aught remained legible; if so, she handed the leaf back to the scribe, who entered the contents into a big book. He looked cross and discontented when all his trouble was wasted, and not a sign remained visible on the page. From time to time the goddess turned towards Ginnistan and the children, and sprinkled them with a few drops of water from the vase. If a drop touched them, it spread into a blue mist, reflecting a thousand gay and pleasant pictures. If a drop fell on the scribe, it changed into countless ciphers and geometrical figures, which he hastily fastened to a thread, and hung round his neck. The boy's mother, a vision of beauty and fascination, often appeared. She was very busy, and often carried away some piece of furniture, which elicited a sharp and angry reproach from the scribe; but no one minded him. At times the mother would nurse little Fable; but as soon as she was called away, Ginnistan took and dandled her, and the child seemed to like her best. Once the father brought in a small ironrod, which he had found in the fields. The scribe looked at it, twisted it about, fastened it to a thread, and showed how it always turned to the north. Ginnistan took it in her hand, breathed on it, and gave it the form of a serpent, biting its tail. The scribe soon tired of observing it, and wrote down an elaborate account of its uses. What was his annoyance, when the leaves came out of the vase as white as snow. Ginnistan went on playing with it, touching the cradle from time to time. The boy woke, threw back the gay curtain, held up one hand to shade his eyes, and held out the other for the serpent.

As soon as he grasped it, he sprang deftly from the cradle, to Ginnistan's amazement, and stood up, clothed only in his long golden hair. The scribe nearly fell from his chair with horror at the sight. Meantime, the child played with the toy, which in his chubby hand turned to the north. As he held it, he grew visibly.

"Sophia," he said to the goddess by the altar, "let me drink out of the vase." She held it out to him, but though he drank eagerly, the contents never diminished. At last he gave it back, and embraced the noble woman. He then coaxed Ginnistan to give him her shawl, of which he made a girdle. He took Fable in his arms. She seemed delighted, and began to talk. Ginnistan made much of him, and pressed him tenderly to her heart; she beckoned to him to follow her, but Sophia shook her head and pointed to the serpent. His mother entered the room; he ran up to her and welcomed her with tearful eyes. The scribe went angrily away. Then came the father, who, when he saw his wife wrapped up in the sight of her boy, caressed Ginnistan behind her back. Little Fable took up the scribe's pen, and began to write. Sophia descended the stair. After a time she returned; the scribe also came back, and drove away Fable with many threatening words. Angrily he gave Sophia the scribbled leaves to wash; but his annoyance was untold when they emerged distinct and legible from the mysterious vase.

Fable clung to her mother, who took her in her arms, while she dusted the room, opened the windows to let in fresh air, and prepared a luxurious meal

Through the window one could see a lovely prospect and a cloudless sky. The father was busily employed in the courtyard. When he was tired, he looked up at the window where Ginnistan sat, and she threw him sweetmeats. The mother and son went out to prepare for their project.

The scribe wrote on, appealing from time to time to Ginnistan, whose memory never failed her.

At last Eros returned in a full suit of armour, round which he had wound Ginnistan's shawl as a scarf. He begged Sophia's advice as to the journey he was about to undertake.

The scribe officiously offered his services to draw out a map of the route, but no one paid attention to him.

"Go at once; let Ginnistan accompany you," said Sophia. "She knows the road, and has many friends. She will assume your mother's form. When you find the King, remember me, and I will come and help you."

Ginnistan assumed the mother's semblance, which seemed to please the father much. The scribe rejoiced at their departure, especially as Ginnistan gave him her handkerchief as a farewell gift. Upon it were recorded the chronicles of the house. But little Fable remained like a thorn in his eye, and he would have willingly seen her join the travelling party. Sophia gave the travellers her blessing, and a phial of the mystic water. The mother was very sad. Fable clamoured to go too. The father alone seemed to take no interest in the matter.

It was night when they set off. The moon stood high in the heaven.

"Dear Eros," said Ginnistan, "we must hurry on to my father, who has long been seeking for me on earth. Do you see his pale, careworn face?"

Eros was touched at the loving meeting between the father and daughter. At last the old man noticed him, and welcomed him heartily. Seizing a mighty horn, he blew a loud blast. The echoes resounded through the ancient walls, and the high towers, with their shining roofs, seemed to bow. Servants streamed forth from all sides. Their strange forms and costumes amused Ginnistan, and did not alarm brave Eros.

Ginnistan greeted all her old friends. The wild Spirit of Springtide was followed by his gentler brother Ebb, old Whirlwind, and passionate Earthquake; nor did the tender Lunar Rainbow fail to appear; while Thunder roared out his complaints about the erratic behaviour of his companion Lightning.

The two lovely sisters Morning and Evening rejoiced over the arrival of the new-comers, and wept softly as they embraced them. It was a marvellous Court that King Moon held. He seemed never weary of looking at his daughter, and she was enchanted with the old familiar scenes and the many quaint things which surrounded her. She joyfully received from her father the key of his treasure-room; he also permitted her to arrange a play to divert Eros during his stay.

The treasure-room was an immense garden, whose countless riches were beyond description. Strange, fantastic palaces, one more gorgeous than another, rose among the clouds. Flocks of sheep, with gold, silver, and rosy fleeces, wandered about, and the strangest animals gave animation to the scene. Here and there were glorious pictures, strange equipages, and brilliant ornaments. The flower-beds glistened with gay flowers. The buildings were crowded with weapons of every kind, soft carpets, artistic tapestries, curtains, vases, goblets, and every kind of beautiful fabric, in richest profusion.

From a rising ground one looked down on a picturesque region, dotted with towns, castles, and temples, and offering all the beauties of cultivation, together with the wildest Alpine solitudes. The distance faded into soft hues of blue, beyond which was a glimpse of a mighty ocean, on whose bosom floated countless snowy-sailed vessels.

The mountain tops shone like fire under their snow and ice; the plains were the softest green. In one direction was pictured a merry-making of happy countryfolk; in another, the outbreak of a volcano, carrying death and devastation in all directions; while two lovers were enjoying the shade of a thick forest, a furious battle seemed raging in a plain beneath them.

These scenes dissolved perpetually into some fresh form. At times portraying some woeful event: parents weeping over the bier of their only son, changing rapidly into a lovely group of children playing round their mother, while an angel smiled at them from the branches of an ancient tree.

To this succeeded a scene of horror and terror. A mighty voice called to arms. Down from the mountains poured a terrific horde of skeletons waving black banners, bent on destroying all life and prosperity, and overran the smiling plain. A terrific struggle ensued, the earth trembled, storms raged, terrific meteors flashed through the black darkness of the sky. The grisly phantoms inflicted death in its most cruel form on all who opposed them, hurling their bodies on an immense funeral pyre, where fire devoured all the children of life.

Suddenly an opalescent light shone around; the phantoms turned to flee, but a rising flood arrested their steps, and engulfed the horrid brood.

All that was terrible vanished away. Heaven and earth united in sweetest harmony. A beauteous blossom floated on the face of the waters. A dazzling rainbow spanned the waves; and godlike forms sat thereon, on glittering thrones.

Sophia sat at the summit, holding the mystic vase; beside her was a noble man, his head wreathed with oak leaves, a palm branch in his hand. A lily leaf bent over the floating blossom, and on it sat Fable, singing sweet songs to the sound of her lyre. Eros himself knelt mid the petals of the flower, at the feet of a slumbering maiden. The petals surrounded them, so that they seemed a part of the flower.

Eros thanked Ginnistan for the strange and enchanting spectacle. Wearied with the journey, and the novel and strange experiences, he longed for rest. Ginnistan led him to a bath, which restored all his strength and vigour; and lying down, he was soon wrapped in sleep.

In the meantime, sad changes had taken place at his home. The scribe stirred up the menials to revolt. He had long been seeking occasion to seize the management of the house. Now he had found his opportunity. The mother was bound in chains, the father imprisoned, and fed on bread and water. Little Fable, hearing the uproar, crouched behind the altar. She saw a door behind it, opened it noiselessly, and descended a gloomy stair. Just then the scribe rushed in to take revenge on Fable and Sophia. Neither were to be seen. The mystic vase was gone. In his fury he broke the altar to fragments, without discovering the secret door.

Fable descended stair after stair. At last she emerged in an open space, surrounded by a colonnade and shut in with gates. It was dusky, the air was full of shadows, and instead of the sun, a black and brilliant body hung in the sky. Still, it was easy to distinguish objects; for every object cast light behind it, instead of shade. Light and shadow had exchanged their tasks. Fable was charmed to be in a new world. She looked around with childish curiosity. At last she reached the gate, where lay a beautiful Sphinx on a massive pedestal.

"What do you seek?" said the Sphinx.

"My own property," replied Fable.

"Whence came you?"

"From the olden time."

"You are a child, and will be ever a child. Who takes care of you?"

"I take care of myself. Where are your sisters?" asked Fable.

"Everywhere, and nowhere," replied the Sphinx.

"Do you know me?"

"Not yet."

"Where is Love?"

"In the imagination."

"And Sophia?"

The Sphinx murmured some incomprehensible words, and fluttered her wings.

"Sophia and Love," exclaimed Fable, triumphantly, and passed through the gate. She entered an immense cavern, and went gaily up to the old sisters, who pursued their strange occupation by the light of a smoky lamp. They paid no attention to the caresses of their little visitor.

At last one of them croaked out in a rough voice, while she turned her squinting eyes upon her –

"What do you want, lazybones? Who let you in? Your silly frolics shake the quiet flame, and waste the oil. Can't you sit down and do something?"

"Pretty cousin, I don't like to be lazy. I could not help laughing at your portress. She tried to kiss me, but she was so heavy she could not get up. Let me sit at the door and spin, for I can't see well here; and while I spin I must chat and laugh, and that might disturb you."

"Out you shall not go; but in the next room a ray from the upper world streams through a cleft in the rocks, there you may spin, if you can. Here are quantities of old ends, spin them together. But beware, if you are careless, or break the thread, it will twine round your neck and choke you."

The old woman laughed spitefully, and span on. Fable picked up an armful of odds and ends, took a spindle and distaff, and ran singing into the next room. Up through the clefts she saw the star Phoenix. Pleased at the good omen, she began to spin and sing. The spindle twisted rapidly as her clever fingers drew the fine, light thread. As she sang, countless will-o'-the-wisps darted through the doorway, and spread through the cavern as hideous sprites and imps.

Meantime, the old women span on, expecting every moment to hear Fable scream. How horrified they were when, all at once, a long nose peered over their shoulders; and when they looked round, they saw a swarm of hideous gnomes and imps, playing hideous pranks. They held on to each other and yelled. Fear would have turned them to stone, if the scribe had not suddenly entered, bearing a branch of mandrake. The will-o'-the-wisps crept into the crevice of the rocks, and the cavern grew light, because, in the confusion, the smoky lamp had been upset. Great as was the old women's joy at recognizing the scribe, still greater was their wrath with Fable. They called her out, scolded her furiously, and forbade her to spin. The scribe looked sneeringly at her, for now he thought she was in his power.

"I am rejoiced to see you here," he said, "and hope you have to work hard, and are well punished. Your good genius led you here. I wish you a long life and a great deal of pleasure." "Thanks," replied she. "You, too, seem to be in luck; if you had but your scythe and your hour-glass, you would seem my pretty cousins' own brother. If you want goose-quills, you might pluck them from their cheeks."

The scribe seemed about to seize her, but she smiled and said –

"If you value your hair and your eyes, beware of my nails."

The scribe turned spitefully to the old women, who were seeking everywhere for their distaffs, for now that the lamp had gone out they could not see. He poured out his wrath about Fable. "Send her to collect tarantulas to make your oil. I must tell you, for your comfort, that Eros is flying about in all directions, and will give your scissors enough to do. His mother, who so often forced you to spin the thread longer, will be burnt to-morrow." He laughed when he saw Fable weep at his news. Then he gave some mandrake to the old women, and went off with his nose in the air.

With an angry voice the old women desired Fable to hunt for tarantulas. She hurried off, pretended to open the door and bang it to, then glided in the dark to the back of the cavern, where she had caught sight of a ladder. Climbing rapidly up, she reached a trapdoor leading to King Arctur's hall.

The King sat in council when Fable entered. On his head sparkled the northern crown; he held a lily in his left hand, scales in his right. At his feet crouched a lion and an eagle.

"All hail, great King!" said Fable, bowing deeply before him. "I bring good news for thy wounded heart. The speedy return of Wisdom, the everlasting presence of Peace, an end to hopeless Love, and a return of the olden days."

The King touched her forehead with the lily. "Ask what boon you like, it shall be granted."

"I crave three: when I beg for the fourth time, Love will be at the gate. Now, give me the lyre."

"Eridanus, bring it," said the King.

Fable struck some harmonious chords; the King handed her a golden beaker, from which she sipped; then she glided over the frozen lake, making music as she went. The ice gave forth melody as she passed, and the rocks responded with glee, taking it as the sound of home-comers.

Fable soon reached the city. There she met her mother, who looked pale and worn, thin and grave. Her beautiful features bore the impress of hopeless sorrow and trusting faith.

"Dear mother, where have you been?" cried Fable. "You are quite changed. How I have longed for you!"

Ginnistan caressed her, and looked pleased and happy. "I thought," said she, "that the scribe could not keep you a prisoner.

The sight of you refreshes me. Things have gone badly with me, but I shall find comfort. Eros is at hand; and when he sees you, he will come and talk to you, and perhaps stay. Since he went with me to my father's Court, long silver-white wings have grown from his shoulders. The strength which developed so suddenly seems now all centred in his wings, and he has again become a boy. The noble glow of enthusiasm in his countenance has faded into a capricious gleam, like a will-o'-the-wisp; his sweet gravity has changed into mere roguishness, and his noble calm into childish caprice."

"I was devoted to the wayward boy, and felt keenly his altered mood, his laughing scorn, and his indifference to my wishes. My appearance has altered, my cheerfulness has fled, and given place to sadness and dread. I could not bear to meet his cruel eyes. I had no other desire but to cure him of his faults; yet I loved him deeply in spite of them. Since he fled from me, in spite of all my entreaties, I have followed him ceaselessly. He does nothing but mock me; when I come up to him, he flies off, and laughs at me. His arrows deal sorrow and pain. I have enough to do to comfort those he has wounded; though I need comfort myself I find his track by the wails of his victims, who mourn bitterly when I leave them. The scribe follows us, taking cruel vengeance on the wounded."

Eros is ever surrounded by a crowd of winged children, who tease all those who have been struck with his arrows.

"See, there they come! I must go; farewell, sweet child! May success ever attend you."

Eros flew on without noticing Ginnistan, but turned to Fable, while his attendant sprites frolicked round her. Fable rejoiced at the sight of her brother, and sang a merry song to her lyre. Eros threw down his bow. His attendant sprites fell asleep on the soft grass. Ginnistan now caught and caressed him, till he too began to nod, and fell asleep with his head on her lap, spreading his wings round her. The weary Ginnistan never took her eyes off the beautiful sleeper. While Fable sang, tarantulas came from every side, bringing their shining webs with them, and dancing in time to the music. Fable comforted her mother, and promised her speedy help. The rocks repeated the soft melody, and lulled the sleeper. Ginnistan sprinkled a few drops from the precious phial, and the sweetest dreams fell upon him. Fable took the phial, and continued her journey; but as she went she played and the tarantulas followed her.

In the distance flames rose high above a mighty forest. Fable looked sadly upwards, till she was soothed by the sight of Sophia's blue veil floating over the earth, and clothing the mighty vault.

The sun rose blood-red with fury; as the flames rose more and more menacing, they seemed to absorb its light, which waned paler and paler. Soon the glory of the day-star faded away before the envious violence of the earthly fire. At last the brilliant orb became a mere burnt-out cinder, and fell into the sea. By this time the flames were resplendent, rising higher and higher towards the North. Fable entered her home, which lay in ruins; thorns and brambles grew in every chink, reptiles of all kinds crawled over the broken steps. She heard a terrible noise within. The scribe and his comrades, who had been exulting over the mother's fiery death, had been terrified by the falling of the sun.

In vain had they striven to extinguish the fire; in their efforts they had been severely burned. Pain and fear forced from them exclamations of rage and complaint.

They were still more alarmed when Fable entered, and rushed towards her to wreak their wrath, but she slipped aside behind the cradle, and they stepped right among the tarantula webs. The furious spiders bit right and left, and the whole crowd began to dance, while Fable struck up a merry air. Laughing at their comical grimaces, she went up to the ruined altar, and, shoving the debris on one side, descended the secret stair, followed by her tarantulas.

The Sphinx called out, "What is more sudden than lightning?"

"Revenge," said Fable.

"What vanishes most quickly? "

"Unjust possessions."

"Who understands the world?"

"He who knows himself."

"What is the eternal secret? "

"Love."

"Who keeps the secret?"

"Sophia."

The Sphinx moaned as Fable entered the cavern.

"Here, I have brought you your tarantulas," said Fable to the old women, who had again lighted their lamp, and were hard at work.

They started up in terror; one of them ran forward to stab her with her scissors. She stumbled over a tarantula, which stung her in the foot. She screamed, the others came to the rescue, and shared her fate. It was impossible for them to seize Fable, as they whirled round and round in giddy dance.

"Make haste," they cried to the little one, "spin us some thin ball dresses, for we are dying of heat in these stiff, heavy ones. You must moisten the thread with spider juice, lest it tear, and work in fire-flowers; or else we will kill you."

"Willingly," said Fable, passing into the next room; "I will give you three plump flies," she said to the spiders, who had fastened their dainty webs to the roof and sides of the cavern, "if you will weave at once three light ball dresses. I will bring you the flowers, which must be interwoven with them, very shortly."

The spiders were soon ready, and began their work. Fable slipped up the ladder to the hall of Arctur.

"O King!" she cried, "the wicked are dancing, the good resting. Has the flame reached you?"

"It has," replied the King. "The night is passed, the ice is melting. My wife is at hand. My enemy is ruined. Everything revives. I cannot yet show myself, as alone I am no King. Speak, what is your boon?"

"I crave some fire-flowers," said Fable. "I know you have a clever gardener who can raise them."

"Zink," called the King, "give us the flowers."

The gardener came forward with a pot full of fire, in which he strewed some seed. In a short time the flowers shot up. Fable gathered an apron full, and set off.

The spiders had been hard at work. Nothing was wanted but to fasten on the flowers, which they did with taste and dexterity. Fable was careful not to break the threads which hung from the weavers.

She carried the dresses to the dancers, who had sunk down overpowered with fatigue from their recent exertions.

She quickly dressed the haggard old women, who scolded her fiercely all the time. Their new dresses were very neatly made, and fitted well. All this time Fable kept soothing and flattering the old witches, praising their work and their attractions. In the meantime they rested, then sprang up to resume the dance with greater vigour than before, wishing the little one a long life and great rewards in rather sarcastic accents. Fable now returned to the spiders. "Eat your flies in peace." But the spiders were so excited by the dancing of the old women, to whose dresses they were still fastened, that they rushed upon them. The old women would have defended themselves with their scissors, but Fable had taken them away. Unable to protect themselves, they were soon overcome by the savage spiders, who sucked out the last drop of their blood and marrow.

Fable looked up through the cleft, and saw Perseus, with his great iron shield. The scissors flew of their own accord towards the shield, and Fable entreated him to cut off Eros' wings, and to immortalize the sisters on his shield, so as to complete the great work.

She then took leave of the underground kingdom, and ascended blithely to Arctur's palace.

"The flax is spun. The dead have lost their power. The living will rule and use all things. The hidden will be manifested, and the seen hidden. The curtain is about to rise on a new scene. Yet once more I crave a boon, then I will sit and spin to all eternity."

"Happy child," said the monarch, "you have delivered us."

"I am only the adopted child of Sophia," said the little one. "Allow me to take Turmalin, the gardener, and Gold, and go to gather my mother's ashes. Earth must no longer remain a chaos."

The King summoned all three, and bade them accompany Fable.

The town was illuminated, the streets were thronged. The lake broke in murmuring waves on the rocky shore as Fable drove past in the royal carriage. Turmalin carefully collected the ashes. They went round the world, till they came to the old giant, down whose shoulders they climbed. He seemed half paralysed, and could scarcely move his limbs. Gold laid a coin in his mouth, and Fable touched his eyes and poured the phial of mystic water on his forehead. As it trickled down his face, a spark of life seemed to stir his frame. He opened his eyes and sprang up. Fable hastened to join her companions on the rising earth, and wished him good morning.

"Are you there, dear child?" said he. "I have long been dreaming of you. I thought you would appear before my eyes and the earth grew heavy. I have slept long."

"The earth is again light, as it was in the good old days," said Fable. "The old days are returning. Soon you will be among old friends. I will spin you merry days; you shall have a helper to share in your joy, and whom you can inspire with youth and strength. Where are our old guests the Hesperides?"

"With Sophia. Their garden will soon bloom again, and perfume the air with its golden fruit They are collecting the withered plants."

Fable hurried to her old home. It was a complete ruin, covered with ivy. The court was overgrown with bushes, and every step carpeted with moss. She entered the hall. Sophia stood by the newly-built altar. Eros lay at her feet, clad in armour, nobler and graver than of yore. A splendid lustre hung from the ceiling. The floor was paved with mosaics of precious stones. Round the altar was a circle of mysterious symbols. Ginnistan bent and wept over a sofa, on which the father reclined. Her blooming countenance wore an expression of thought and love, which enhanced its beauty.

Fable handed the urn containing the sacred ashes to Sophia, who embraced her tenderly.

"Dearest child, your zeal and faith have won you a place amid the eternal stars. You have chosen the undying portion, the Phoenix is yours. You will be the soul of your life. Now wake up the bridegroom. The herald calls; 'Eros must go and seek Freya.'"

Fable rejoiced at these words. She called Gold and Zink, and approached the couch. Ginnistan watched anxiously. Gold melted a coin, and a shining stream poured over the sleeping form; Zink fastened a chain round Ginnistan's neck. The waters rose, both bodies floated on the shining stream.

"Stoop down, dear mother, and lay your hand on his heart," said Fable.

Ginnistan did so. She saw her reflection in the stream. The chain touched the stream, her hand lay on his heart, he started from his sleep, and pressed his bride in his arms.

The metal ran into the shape of a mirror. The father rose from his long sleep, his eyes shone, and his whole form had the grace and elasticity of youth and strength.

The happy pair approached Sophia, who spoke words of blessing, and admonished them ever to consult the mirror, which reflected everything in its genuine shape, and destroyed all hurtful illusions.

She then took the ashes and poured them into the vase on the altar. A soft murmur was heard and a gentle breeze stirred the hair and robes of all present.

Sophia handed the vase to Eros, and he offered it to the others. All tasted the divine contents, and felt calm and refreshment steal into their hearts. The mother's presence seemed among them, her spirit permeated their very being.

Their highest expectations were more than fulfilled. All saw what had hitherto been wanting in their lives. The room seemed to them a hallowed spot.

"The great secret is now revealed," said Sophia, "but remains unfathomable. The new world rises from pain, and eternity is revealed to tears. The heavenly mother lives in each of her children. Do you not feel the new life within you?"

She poured out the contents of the vase. The earth trembled.

"Eros," said Sophia, "go with your sister to your bride. You shall soon see me again."

Fable and Eros hastened away. A glorious spring spread over the earth. Everything throbbed with life. The moon and the clouds hurried northwards. The royal palace cast its radiant effulgence far over the sea. The King and his retinue stood on the battlements. Everywhere were seen crowds of familiar forms converging to one point. Bands of youths and maidens shouted welcome as they approached the royal abode. In all directions were seen newly awakened couples, holding one another in close embrace, and looking with surprise and wonder at the new world. Flowers and trees sprang up with undreamt of vigour. Everything was full of life. Everyone spoke and sang. Fable greeted countless old friends. The plants exhaled the richest perfume; the trees were laden with fruit, All burdens had fallen from every heart. They reached the lake. A light skiff lay moored to the shore; they went on board, and turned the prow northwards. The vessel shot through the waves like an arrow. They hastened up the broad stairs. Eros was amazed at the magnificence of all around him. The frozen cascade had regained its motion in the garden, and diffused fresh life and beauty among the flowers.

The old hero met them at the gate.

"Worthy old man," said Fable, "Eros requires a sword. Gold gave him a chain, one end of which is fastened to the bottom of the sea, the other is attached to his breast. Take hold of it, and let us lead him to the hall where the Princess rests."

Eros took a sword from the old man's hand, holding the hilt to his heart, and pointing it before him.

The folding doors flew open. Eros approached the slumbering Princess. Suddenly there was a mighty crash. A spark, emanating from Freya, struck the point of the sword; both sword and chain flashed fire.

The old hero supported Fable, who had fallen backward with fright. "Throw away your sword," she cried, "and waken the Princess." Eros cast it from him, hastened up to Freya, and kissed her sweet lips. She opened her dark eyes, and knew her lover. A long kiss cemented the eternal bond.

The King, leading Sophia, descended from the cupola. The stars and the spirits of nature followed in a never-ending procession. An inexpressibly brilliant light flooded the hall, the palace, the town, and the heavens. Countless multitudes thronged in to see the lovers, who knelt before the King and Queen for their blessing. The King took off his diadem, and placed it on the golden locks of Eros. The old hero took off his armour, and the King threw a royal mantle over him. Then he placed a lily in his left hand and Sophia clasped a sparkling bracelet round the lovers' joined hands, while she placed a crown on Freya's brown hair.

"All hail to our old rulers!" shouted the people.

"They have been with us all along, but we knew them not. Hail, all hail! Rule us for ever! Bless us also!"

Sophia spoke to the new-crowned Queen, "Throw your bracelet in the air, so that the world and the nations may be bound to you for aye."

The bracelet whirled through the air, melting as it flew. Haloes of light shone round every head, and a dazzling bond joined town and lake with the earth in its new, glorious spring.

Perseus now appeared, bearing a spindle and a basket. He offered it to the new King.

"Here," said he, "is all that remains of your enemy."

A stone tablet, marked out with black and white chequers, lay in the basket, and curious figures formed of spotless alabaster and black marble.

"It is a game of chess," said Sophia. "For the future, there will be no war except on this board, and with these figures. It is a remembrance of the sad old days of strife."

Perseus turned to Fable, and gave her the distaff and spindle. "In your hands this distaff will yield a golden and imperishable thread."

The Phoenix flew to her feet, and spread out its wings, on which she took her seat, and was raised above the throne. Here she sang a divine song, spinning diligently all the time, and drawing out the thread from her breast.

The people shouted with joy, and all eyes were fastened on the marvellous child.

A fresh burst of applause rose from the gates. The old King

entered with his strange retinue; behind him Ginnistan and her bridegroom were borne in triumph. They were wreathed in flowers. The royal family greeted them tenderly, and the new King and Queen named them their viceregents on earth.

"Grant me the realms of the Fates," said the Moon. "Their abode has just risen above ground in the strange palace gardens, there little Fable and I will entertain you with plays."

The King agreed; Fable nodded her concurrence; and the people rejoiced at the prospect of such amusement. The Hesperides came in their turn to offer their congratulations, and beg for protection for their garden. Countless deputations succeeded, all offering heartfelt wishes to the newly-married pair.

The King embraced his bride; all present followed his example, and embraced each other. Nothing was heard but the murmur of loving words and kisses.

At last Sophia said, "The mother is amongst us. Her presence ensures perpetual happiness. Follow us to the temple; there we will ever dwell and preserve the secret of the world."

Fable span more swiftly than ever, and sang –

"Gone is the age of strife,
All sadness passed away.
Now has begun celestial life,
All own Sophia's sway."

# SECOND PART

# FULFILMENT

A PILGRIM, lost in deep thought, slowly ascended a narrow, rugged path among the mountains. Midday was past. A rushing wind drove the fleecy clouds through the sky. Many voices sounded in the blast, voices which awoke echoes in the heart – but the pilgrim heeded them not. He reached the summit of the hill, where he hoped to find his goal. Hoped? Alas! he no longer hoped. Anguish and despair drove him up the roughest paths of the mountains, that bodily fatigue might deaden the bitterness of his soul. He was wearied and silent. He rested on a stone, without observing aught around him. He felt as if in a dream, and as if all life had been only a dream. An indescribable glory seemed suddenly revealed to him. He burst into a flood of tears, and sobbed bitterly. The outbreak of grief relieved his broken heart: happier thoughts and old memories awoke in his breast.

Below him lay Augsburg, with its towers; far in the distance gleamed the mysterious stream: the gloomy far-stretching forest and the jagged line of mountain seemed keeping eternal watch over it, and both appeared to say, "Hurry as you like, O stream, you shall not escape us; winged ships shall follow you, and I will

bar your way, and hide you in my bosom. Trust to us, pilgrim –
he is our enemy, too; let him hurry on with his prey, yet he shall
not escape."

The poor pilgrim recalled the olden days, and their vanished
delights; his soul fainted at their memory. His broad hat sheltered
a youthful face, but it was pale and thin; tears had quenched the
keen joy of life, his lightly drawn breath had turned to sighs, all
the bright colours of life had faded into ashen-grey.

Suddenly he perceived the figure of a monk kneel in prayer at
the foot of a mighty oak. Was it the old Chaplain? The nearer he
approached, the bigger seemed the monk, until he saw his
mistake: a fantastic rock had deceived his eyes. Full of emotion,
he pressed his head on the cold stone, and throwing his arm
round it, he wept aloud, "Oh that the Holy Mother would give
me a sign! I am so sad and lonely, will no kind saint intercede for
me? Pray for me, dear father."

As he uttered these words the oak shivered; the rocks groaned;
and clear, silvery voices rose from far below singing,

"Naught knows she now but peace and rest;
Banished all grief and woe.
She holds her infant to her breast,
And murmurs sweet and low –
"Pass quickly time, oh I pass away,
And bring him, too, to endless day."

The low, clear voices rang out exultingly, then ceased. All was
again silent, then the amazed pilgrim heard someone in the tree
say –

"If you will play a song in my honour on your lute, a poor
maiden will come to you. Take her with you, and do not let her
go. When you reach the Emperor, remember me. I have chosen
this place to live here with my child. Build us a good, warm
house. My little child has overcome death. Do not grieve, I am
with you. You must still abide awhile on earth; but the maiden
will comfort you, until you, too, die and rejoin your friends."

"It is Matilda's voice," cried the pilgrim, falling on his knees. A ray of light fell on him through the branches, and he perceived far away an indescribable scene of beatitude. Light, airy figures, with beautiful, calm, and loving faces, greeted one another with winning gestures. Among them stood the pilgrim's beloved Matilda.

She appeared as though she would speak to him, but he could hear nothing. He looked at her lovely features with deep longing, as she signed to him and laid her hand on her heart. The vision comforted and refreshed his weary soul. Long after it had vanished, he remained kneeling in holy contemplation. The heavenly vision had drawn all sadness and bitterness from his soul: his heart was again light and free, his spirit revived, and filled with fresh energy. No sorrow, save an unutterable longing, remained. The wild pangs of loneliness and despair, the horrible oppression and weariness had departed, and the pilgrim could again look around him and take an interest in life. His voice, his words were set free as from a spell; his thoughts were deeper. Death had brought to him a revelation of life, and he could think with childlike confidence of his own short span of existence. The future and the past seemed all that belonged to him. He stood apart from the present a stranger to the world, who had but to traverse her gay halls for a short space.

It was evening; earth seemed to him like an old home, to which he was returning. A thousand memories rose up before him; every stone, every tree, every hill, recalled past days; and as he went along he sang.

When he looked up he discerned a young maiden standing near him, by a rock. She greeted him as an old acquaintance, and invited him to her house, where she had prepared supper for him. She begged him excuse her delaying a moment; and he watched her go to the tree, look upward with a smiling face, then throw a shower of roses on the grass, out of her apron. She knelt beside them for a moment, then rose and came to the pilgrim.

"Who told you about me?" said he.

"Our Mother."

"Who is your mother?"

"The Holy Mother."

"How long have you been here?"

"Since I left the grave."

"Have you passed through death?"

"How else could I live?"

"Do you live here all alone?"

"There is an old man in the house, but I know many who have lived."

"Are you inclined to stay with me?"

"Yes, I love you."

"How do you know me?"

"I have known you long, and my mother often spoke of you."

"Have you a mother?"

"Yes."

"What is her name?"

"Maria."

"Who was your father?"

"The Graf von Hohenzollern."

"I know him."

"So you ought, for he is your father too."

"My father lives at Eisenach."

"You have other parents."

"Where are we going?"

"Home."

At last they reached a glade in the forest. In front of them were some ruined towers, surrounded by a moat. Bushes grew on the crumbling walls, like a garland on some white-headed sire. As they looked at the hoary stones and the yawning crevices, they seemed carried back to primeval times; and strange stories of the past flashed before them instantaneously. Even as when one looks up into the deep, soft blue of a summer-night sky, and marks the milky glimmer, innocent-looking as an infant's cheek, which recalls the existence of stupendous spheres. They passed under an old gateway, and the pilgrim looked with surprise at the magnificent and unknown flowers and plants which clothed the ruins. At a little distance rose a small, stone-built cottage with large windows.

An old man stood behind some broad-leaved plants fastening the tender branches to supports. The maiden led him forward, saying, "Here is Heinrich, whom you have so often asked for."

As the old man turned to him, Heinrich thought he recognized the old miner's face. "You see doctor Sylvester," said the maiden.

Sylvester greeted him kindly. "It is a long time since I saw your father. He was then about your age. I made him acquainted with the treasures of the past, the rich inheritance bequeathed by too quickly passing ages. I saw in him the signs of a great artist: his eye was quick and bright, the eye of perception; his face showed perseverance and firmness; but the present world had taken too deep root in his nature, he would not listen to his better self. The cold severity of his native skies checked the tender shoots of a nobler growth. He became a dexterous artist, and deemed all enthusiasm folly."

"I have often seen a secret sadness in him," replied Heinrich. "He worked ceaselessly, more out of habit than from pleasure. In spite of his peaceful life, the comforts he enjoyed, the honour in which he was held by his fellow-citizens, who sought his advice in all difficulties – there was something ever wanting, which these could not replace. His friends thought he was very happy, and knew not how weary of life he was, how empty the world seemed to him, and that it was not from love of gain, but to scare away discontent, that he worked so ceaselessly."

"What surprised me most," said Sylvester, "was that he left your education so entirely in your mother's hands, carefully avoiding all responsibility as to your future career. Happily, you grew up free from injurious restraint on the part of your parents, for most people resemble the relics of a rich banquet, which has been plundered by men of opposite tastes."

"All that I know about education," said Heinrich, "is from

❖ 153

watching the life and character of my father and mother, and what I learnt from the Court Chaplain. My father's calm, firm opinions, which made him judge all events on the same principles as if they had been works of art, had, unknown to him, a great effect on me. Joined to this, he held in deep reverence all the mysterious and inexplicable influences which surround us; and, with modest self-denial, refrained from interfering with the development of his child's character. He thought here is a busy, enquiring nature, fresh from the unknown source of life; it bears the impress of a wondrous world, no earthly current has carried it away, and obliterated its natural impulses or destroyed its devout musings on the unseen; it is in the same state as men in those happy early ages when the world was young and bright, and the spirit of revelation accompanied their steps with an almost visible presence."

"Sit here on this bench, beneath the flowers," said the old man; "Cyane will call us when supper is ready; and may I beg you to continue the story of your life. We old people love to hear of the years of childhood; they exhale a rare perfume like that of a flower."

"First, tell me how do you like my hermitage, and my garden, for these flowers are my friends? All those you see love me, as I love them; I am here among my children like an old tree round whose roots rise youth and gaiety."

"Happy father," replied Heinrich, "your garden is like the world. Ruins have given birth to these blooming children; this lovely creation draws its support from the relics of past ages. But must the mother die that the children may flourish; and is the father condemned to sit and weep by her grave?"

Sylvester held out his hand to the sobbing youth, and rose to fetch him a forget-me-not bound to a cypress branch. The wind moaned in the tops of the pines on the other side of the ruins. Heinrich hid his tear-bathed face on Sylvester's shoulder; when he again looked up, the evening star was rising gloriously over the dark forest.

After a pause, Sylvester resumed. "I should like to have seen you among your play-fellows at Eisenach. Your parents, the excellent Landgrävin, your father's honest neighbours, and the worthy Chaplain, formed a charming group; their conversation must have had a great effect upon you, the more so, as you were an only child. The country, too, was picturesque and attractive."

"I admire it more since I have seen other countries," said Heinrich. "Every plant, tree, hill, and mountain has its own appropriate place, where its peculiar growth and formation is required. Only men and animals can visit all regions and make them theirs. Men who have travelled much, birds of passage, and beasts of prey are distinguished by greater intelligence and wonderful gifts. Of course, some men profit more from travel than others; some men have not the perceptive power and attention which enable them to observe new circumstances with profit to themselves. My fatherland and my early impressions seem to have coloured my life. The more I reflect, the more sure I am that fate and character are interchangeable words."

"Nature has always had a great attraction for me," said Sylvester. "I am never weary of contemplating plants and flowers. The plants of a region are its voice; every fresh leaf and flower has its secret to tell. When one finds an unknown flower in a lonely place, does one not feel it a revelation, and listen for the gentle tones which seem hovering near? One almost weeps with joy, and feels inclined to take root on the spot, so as to remain in such a charming neighbourhood forever. This green, mysterious drapery is drawn over the whole bare, dry earth. Every spring it is renewed, and it speaks to all loving hearts like the flowerlanguage of the East. Every day it teaches a fresh lesson, and manifests more clearly the charm of nature. This is the greatest enjoyment which earth can give; every fresh region explains the fresh riddle of – whence do I come and whither do I go?"

"We were talking," said Heinrich, "of childhood and of education, which your garden, with its innocent blossoms, recalled to our memories. My father is also a devoted gardener, and spends the happiest hours of his life among his flowers. This, no doubt, keeps his heart so open to children, as flowers are but child types. In them we see the glory of eternal life, the mighty powers of coming ages, the world as it may one day be, when all is made new for ever. The mighty power of attraction influences them, as it does animated nature; but their love exhales only in perfume, free from all violence and passion.

"Such should be childhood on earth; but the clouds which sail in their beauty through the cloudless skies, seem revelations of the second and nobler childhood which awaits us in Paradise.

"There is a mystery in clouds," said Sylvester. "Certain clouds have a strange influence upon us. They attract us, and seem as though they would draw us up into their cool and refreshing shade; their forms are gay and lovely, like the visions of our brain, and the brilliant light they cast upon the earth seems a foreshadowing of glory. There are, however, gloomy, awe-inspiring clouds, in which all the terrors of darkness seem to threaten us. The radiant blue is blotted out, it seems as if the skies could never clear again, and the threatening copper-glow on the black background fills all hearts with dread. When the lightning flashes, and the thunder gives one loud, far-echoing peal after another, we might easily believe that we were given over to the power of evil spirits. It is like an echo of old superhuman nature, but it also rouses the divine conscience within. Material nature groans in its foundations, but the spiritual waxes brighter and brighter."

"When will the time come," said Heinrich, "when pain, evil, terror, and sorrow will come to an end?"

"When there is but one power – the power of conscience – when all nature is obedient and orderly. There is but one cause of evil – universal weakness; and this weakness is nothing else than a low moral tone, and want of desire for true freedom."

"Explain the power of conscience to me."

"If I could, I should be God; when you understand it, it exists in you. Could you explain the art of poetry?"

"One cannot explain a personal quality."

"How much less a secret of so high a nature. Can you explain music to the deaf?"

"Is it a key to a new world? Can one only comprehend it because one has it?"

"The universe consists of system within system of mighty worlds. All sciences blend in each other, but each has its own individuality. Providence alone knows what is the connection between our world and the mighty universe. It is difficult even to form an idea as to whether our increase of knowledge in this world is a mere temporary development, or a preparation for higher faculties."

"Perhaps it is both," said Heinrich. "Imagination alone reveals to me what this present world is; even conscience, the germ of all individuality, the enlivening and quickening power, appears to me like the spirit of poetry in life, bringing about strange conjunctions in the varied romance of existence."

"Worthy pilgrim," replied Sylvester, "conscience is seen in every earnest work, and every painfully substantiated truth. All true cultivation leads to freedom. Freedom is mastery. The master is free to choose his subject and his manner of carrying it out. All the conditions of his art are subservient to his will, nothing binds or hinders him. This complete freedom and mastery is the essence of conscience. Every noble, true work is a manifestation of the perfect, complete world – which rose into being at one word of the Almighty."

"Ethics, then," replied Heinrich, "are religion; and science, theology. Do they then but contain laws which bear the same relation to worship as nature does to God: ladders, trains of thought leading upward to the Unseen? May they not also be defined as an analysis of religion, an attempt at settling its relative position to man's personal needs?"

"Conscience," said Sylvester, "represents God upon earth, and is the highest and best of all gifts. How far above either ethics or morality is this pure, all-embracing spirit? Conscience is a revelation of man's highest nature; it cannot be defined as this or that; it speaks no trite language of command; it does not consist in a few virtues. There is but one virtue – the pure, earnest will, which decides at once and irrevocably the cause of truth. It inhabits and animates the human body, and controls every action."

"Father, your words fill me with joy," interrupted Heinrich. "Imagination, then, is but virtue in an attractive form; it is she who animates the art of the poet, and gives colour to life. The poet may, then, safely follow the suggestions of his fancy, or if his mind is raised above the material, the inspirations of higher beings, and give himself up to his work in childlike humility. Religion and virtue are to one another what fancy is to ideal teaching. The Holy Scriptures preserve the records of revelation; and ideality unfolds a higher sphere in countless poems of undying fame. Fable and history are closely intertwined; and the *Bible* and ideality are stars which revolve in the same sphere."

"You speak truly," said Sylvester, "and now you can understand better how science is the spirit of nature. It is the allkindling, animating life. It explains everything, from the stars in your glorious vault to the smallest herb in the meadow, and leads us on through the endless complications of nature to revelation."

"You have satisfied me as to the connection between science and religion. Experience and the teaching of conscience all prove the union of this world with a higher sphere. The more we know, the more clearly religion is unfolded to us; what was at first but the ignorant craving of our nature, becomes then an absolute reality, the only true harmony, the mysterious union of the holy soul with God, His abiding presence and His love animating our inmost being."

"The innocency of your heart makes you a prophet," said Sylvester. "Everything will become clear to you, the world and its history will be transfigured into holy writings, even as from the holy writings you will learn how simply and clearly the greatest Events can be recorded. Perhaps not directly by them, but their elevating and animating influence will arouse a higher faculty within you.

"The love of nature has brought me to the same result to which poetry has led you. Art and history drew me to nature.

"My parents lived in Sicily, not far from the famous Etna. We inhabited an ancient house on the sea-shore, shaded by lofty chestnuts and surrounded by beautiful gardens. Not far off were a cluster of huts belonging to fishermen, vine-dressers, and shepherds. Our house was richly provided with all material comforts, nor were intellectual pleasures wanting. We had many rare sculptures and daintily engraved cameos, together with an accumulated store of parchment rolls, treating of all the varied knowledge of the past.

"My father's reputation as an astrologer brought us many visitors, even from distant lands. As the knowledge of futurity is a rare gift, they deemed it only just to give my father such rich presents as might enable him to pursue his calm and studious life."

*The following summary of the story as it might continue is by Ludwig Tieck:*

The author went no further in his composition of this second part. He called it the Fulfilment, and the first part Expectation. In the second, all that the first shadowed forth was to be made clear.

It was the author's intention, after he had completed *Heinrich von Ofterdingen* to write six other romances, in which he would give his views on physics, higher life, commerce, history, politics, and love, in the same way as he had treated poetry in *Ofterdingen*, Without my pointing it out, the intelligent reader will see that the author did not confine himself strictly to the epoch in which the well-known Minnesänger lived, although everything reminds one of it. It is a great loss, not only to the author's friends, but to art and literature, that he left this work unfinished. Its intentions and great originality would have been seen more clearly in the continuation. He did not merely aim at representing one side of poetry in various human scenes, but at giving a view of what poetry really is in itself.

To achieve this object, he brings in nature, history, war, and social life, because their very life is poetry.

I will make an attempt, as far as I can remember his conversations with me and my friends (with the help of the papers he left behind), to give an idea of the plan and scope of the last portion of his work.

The poet who is inspired by his art is at home everywhere. Nothing strange or repellent; for him all riddles are solved; he is familiar with all ages and worlds; wonders vanish, and everything is transformed into the marvellous. The reader will find the boldest views in the Märchen, which concludes the first part: all distinctions of time and space seem annihilated. The author intended this tale to be the transition to the second part, in which matters of fact were to be blended with the ideal, each explaining the other. At the commencement of each chapter there was to be a poetical prologue. The spirit who speaks in the verses was thus to unite the seen and the unseen. This spirit is poetry, and is at the same time the child born to Heinrich and Matilda.

The gardener with whom Heinrich converses is the same old man whom his father had met years ago. Cyane is not his daughter, but the child of the Graf von Hohenzollern. She came when very young from the East, yet she has not forgotten all about her home. She lived for long a strange life in the mountains. She is bright and cheerful, and quite familiar with wonders. She tells the poet all about his own life. She sends him to a distant monastery, which is inhabited by ghosts, all possessed of strange magic powers. They are the priests who keep alive the holy fire in young hearts. He leaves the mystic chants of the brethren, and has a vision in the church. He talks to an old monk about death, and magic, and the philosopher's stone.

A new period opens in the story: from the silence of death, the Minnesänger passes to the most stirring scenes. He has lived among the dead, and conversed with them. The book was now to become dramatic.

Suddenly Heinrich finds himself in Italy amidst the wildest scenes of war. He takes the command of an army, and attacks a town. All the elements of war are represented in poetical colours.

A love episode is introduced, between a noble Pisan and a maiden of Florence. Numerous war-songs. War was to be presented in its most chivalrous, philosophical, and noble form.

At Pisa, Heinrich meets the Emperor Friederich's son; they become close friends. They go to Loretto. He is driven by a storm to Greece. His mind is full of the old world and its heroes. He talks to an old Greek about morality, sculpture, and ancient history. Conversations on government and mythology.

Having learnt to understand the heroic period and antiquity, Heinrich goes to the East, which he had longed to see from his childhood. He visits Jerusalem, becomes acquainted with Eastern poetry. Curious events connect him with the pagans, and he meets the relations of the girl who had given him the riband. He describes the life of a nomadic tribe, Persian fairy tales, remembrances of a primitive world. Every episode was to recall the fabled blue flower; the most varied events were to be connected, Greek, Oriental, Biblical, and Christian, with reminiscences of Indian and Scandinavian mythologies. The Crusades. Life at sea. Heinrich goes to Rome; then follows Roman history.

Heinrich returns to Germany full of experience. He finds his grandfather and Klingsohr.

He turns his steps to Friederich's Court, and becomes intimate with the Emperor. All the most distinguished and learned men in the world were attracted there. Then follow descriptions of pomp, magnificence, and society. German characters and history are brought out. Heinrich discusses government with the Emperor, and gives the prince ideas; also touches on the tribe of impostors who surround a throne.

After Heinrich's experience of life, death, war, travel, and history, he returns home.

In the collection of the Minnesänger's works, we find a strange, involved poetic contest between Ofterdingen, Klingsohr, and other poets; instead of this, the author describes a strange poetic trial; the singers siding for and against the good and evil principle in poetry, religion, or atheism, the seen, and the unseen.

This is Heinrich's last act on earth, the prelude to his trans-figuration. In the most natural, yet supernatural way, all differences are abolished, everything is explained. The barrier between Fable and Truth, Past and Present is removed. Faith, Imagination and Poetry unfold the ideal world.

Heinrich enters Sophia's country, and finds Nature as she ought to be. He hears an old song which awakens long-forgotten memories. He finds a golden key which had been stolen from him years before by a raven. The key had been given to him, soon after Matilda's death, by an old man, who told him to take it to the Emperor. Heinrich takes it to the Emperor, who gives him in exchange an old parchment, on which was inscribed that it was to be given to a man bearing a golden key. By means of the teaching of the parchment, he sets off to seek a carbuncle which is to fill an empty place in the imperial crown. On the way Heinrich meets the stranger who had first told him of the blue flower. They enter the mountains, followed by Cyane.

Soon he reaches a marvellous country, where air and water, flowers and animals are quite different from those on earth. "Men, beasts, plants, stones, stars, the elements, and the colours act and talk like human beings." He finds the blue flower – it is Matilda, asleep, holding the carbuncle; a little child, his and Matilda's, touches him and rejuvenates him. The child symbolized the golden age.

Heinrich plucks the blue flower, and delivers Matilda from her spell; but he loses her again. Fossilized with grief, he becomes, a stone. Edda (the blue flower, Matilda) offers herself to the stone. He turns into a tree. Cyane hews down the tree, and burns it and herself. He becomes a golden ram. Edda (Matilda) offers him as a sacrifice, and he resumes a human form.

He is perfectly happy with Matilda, who is one and the same as Cyane and the Eastern girl. Magnificent feasts are prepared, death is past, now has come the awaking.

Klingsohr appears as King of Atlantis; Heinrich's mother is Ideality, his father is Reason; Schwaning is the Moon; the miner is the Antiquary, and also the old hero Eisen. Emperor Friedrich is Arctur. Even the Graf von Hohenzllern and the merchants are introduced.

Everything turns into allegory. Cyane takes the carbuncle to the Emperor, and Heinrich is the poet in the fairy tale told by the merchants.

The blessed land undergoes only one more enchantment: it is conquered by the Seasons. Heinrich overthrows the realm of the Sun; and the whole work ends in a great poem, which is left unfinished, "The Marriage of the Seasons."

They visit the Sun and fetch thence Day; then go North to find Winter, South to find Summer; Spring they find in the East, Autumn in the West.

This is about all I can remember. Had all his ideas been worked out, it would have remained an enduring monument of a new form of poetry. My account has been short and dry, lest my own fancy should mislead me. Perhaps the reader may be as much touched with these fragments as I was, and look at them as sadly as he would at a mutilated picture of Raphael or Correggio.

# FUGITIVE THOUGHTS

The art of writing books has not yet been found out. It is, however, near at hand. The fragments which exist are literary seed-beds. Many of the seeds fail; but here and there one will spring up and bear fruit.

> •

In scraps of this kind, it does not do to be too matter of fact. Those who write in that fashion cannot claim the name of authors. Must one always be deliberate? Let him who has no enthusiasm forswear all gatherings of young folks. This is the age of literary saturnalias. The more varied life is, the better.

> •

There is a want of romance and variety of thought (in *Ofterdingen*). An outwardly simple style, romantic and dramatic commencement, continuation and end – now conversation – now speeches – then story mixed with reflections and descriptions. A complete mental picture, where feeling, thought, perception, description, talk, and music are ceaselessly changing place, while each stands out clear and distinct from the whole.

> •

Shakespeare is more obscure to me than any Greek author. I can follow the jokes in Aristophanes, but I cannot make out Shakespeare's quips. Jesting seems to be unnatural and forced in poetry.

•

Perhaps I owe my happiest thoughts to the fact, that impressions do not strike me at once in their full completion, but first enter my brain in an uncertain and tentative form.

•

Goethe is the real king of poetry upon earth.

•

Every work of art is formed of spirit element.

•

One of Goethe's peculiarities is the way in which he connects little, insignificant circumstances with leading ideas. He appears to have no other intention than that of occupying the imagination in a poetic way with mysterious by-play. He has followed Nature in this, and learned her art. Ordinary life is full of such coincidences. Surprises and disappointments form the ground-work of all plays. Many sayings in common life are based upon the observation that the results of an action are in contradiction to the expectations founded on it. So bad dreams betoken luck; a hare crossing the path, misfortune. Almost all the superstitions of the vulgar are built on this principle of contrariety.

•

The poet understands Nature better than the man of science.

•

Fairy tale is the basis of poetry. All poetry must be animated by the fairy ideal. The poet adores fate.

•

Comedy and tragedy gain greatly, and only become true poetry by a symbolical union. There must be gleams of mirth athwart what is serious, and gravity mingled with mirth.

•

The representation of feeling must be like the representation of nature, independent, complete, and original. Not as we find it, but as it ought to be.

•

Poetry heals the wounds given by reason. Its elements are of a totally opposite character, and may be described as elevated truth and agreeable illusion.

•

It is easy to be understood how all things tend to poetry. Is not the whole universe full of soul?

•

Even ordinary work can be treated poetically. The ancients understood this well. How poetically they describe herbs, machines, houses, furniture, & c. A peculiar antiquated phraseology, a right arrangement of subjects, a slight touch of allegory, mystery, reflection, and surprise interwoven with the style – these are the essential elements which I require for my Romance.

•

One must strive to maintain a ceaseless current of thought. If one has no time for a wide view of general literature, free thought, and calm reflection, even the most active imagination will grow dull, and the inward alertness cease. The poet must be alive to all the varying conditions of life with their special peculiarities, and have also a keen interest in all science and knowledge.

•

There are moments when even alphabets and books of reference may appear poetical.

•

A tale may often treat of the commonplace, but it must do so in an amusing way. It keeps imagination on the stretch, awakens a feverish interest, and, if the result is well worked out, leaves the reader satisfied.

•

All poetry forms a contrast to actual humdrum life; and real poetry revives the mind, even as sleep does the body. Illness, strange events, journeys, fresh acquaintances, influence us in the same way.

•

The past history of mankind is like an incomplete poem. Our belief in an ultimate reconciliation is in reality a confidence in the final poetic harmony of life. It is in our own power to tune our highest faculties, and infuse poetry into existence.

•

The artist rises above other men, as the statue does above its pedestal.

•

Poetry is creation. All poems must have a living individuality.

•

The power by which one throws oneself entirely into an extraneous individuality – not merely imitating it – is still quite unknown; it arises from keen perception and intellectual mimicry. The true artist can make himself anything that he likes.

•

Poetry is absolute truth. That is the gist of my philosophy. The more poetic, the more truthful.

•

That teaching falls within the province of art, is abundantly proved by Goethe's observations on the metamorphoses of plants and insects. One may assert confidently that Goethe was the greatest natural philosopher of his age, and his writings formed an epoch in science. There can be no question as to the extent of knowledge or the amount of discoveries requisite to raise a man to the rank of a scientific inquirer into nature. The question is, Whether nature is studied with the same appreciation as an antique? After all, what is nature but – a living antique? Nature and scientific inquiry are on a par with art and artistic comprehension. The study of the antique is only now beginning to take its proper place. A true artist keeps it ever in mind and before his eyes. The fragments handed down to us from past ages are incentives to the cultivation of pure art. They were no material creations of the hands. They are manifestations of spirit power, which has embodied itself in stone and marble. If Goethe surpassed other natural philosophers, so in the same way he excelled other poets.

•

Others have excelled him in extent of knowledge, manysidedness, and reflection; but no one can compare with him in creative power. He achieves, where others attempt. We all strive to create – but how few are original. The philosopher of the schools may call this empiricism.

•

Let us consider Goethe's art-life and his intellects. He analyses with such amazing exactness that the object could be reconstructed from his analysis.

•

This is nothing else than practical philosophy; and, to our: surprise, we find out that he applies practical philosophy as all true artists do. The seat of art is intellect. Intellect creates in accordance with her characteristic perception. Fancy, wit, and judgment are all called into play.

•

*Wilhelm Meister* is a production of art, a creation of the intellect. Many mediocre works of art are admitted into a gallery, while the most perfect literal work is excluded.

•

Italians and Spaniards have much greater artistic talent than we have; even the French are not destitute of art; but the English have much less, and are like us, who seldom possess artistic power, although most richly gifted with all those qualities of intellect which are requisite for art production.

•

This abundance of art essentials makes the few artists who arise among us so original, that we may be certain that the most splendid of all works of art will in time be produced by us, as no nation can compare with us in energy. If I understand our latest authors aright, they uphold the study of the ancients as a means of cultivation, not to make us slavish imitators, but to develop true artistic feeling. No modern nation has such comprehension of art as the ancients. By diligent and thoughtful study of the classics, we shall produce such a literature as never existed in classic ages. Goethe resembles classical writers in strength, but has a higher standard, which, however, is no merit of his. Goethe, however, will, and must, be surpassed; but only as the ancients have been, in power, in breadth of view, and reflection; not in the point of view of pure art, for his justness of observation and strength are even more perfect than they appear to be.

•

Lessing saw individual facts too keenly, to the exclusion of the magical effect of the whole environing circumstances.

•

Voltaire is one of the greatest minus poets that ever lived. His *Candida* is his *Odyssey*. It is to be regretted that his world was a Parisian boudoir; had he had less national and personal vanity, he would have achieved more.

•

The lamentable thing about our Church music is that it expresses merely the religion of the *Old Testament* – a religion of penalties. The *New Testament* is still a sealed book to us. We have, however, some excellent attempts at real spiritual music; for example, "God save the King" and "How sweet they sleep."

•

Arabesques and ornaments are embodied music.

•

Antiques seem almost holy relics.

•

No bungler ever attains to the spirit of any art. He imitates like an ape, but has no comprehension of the essentials of art. The real painter, & c., discerns at once what is picturesque. It is the same as regards the poet and the novel writer. Chroniclers are historydaubers; they try to give too much, and give nothing. Each art has its own sphere; he who cannot discern its limits is no artist.

•

All talents spring from intellect. Intellect sets the task,

imagination chalks out the design, but intellect carries it out.

•

A romance must be like an English garden, every point must tell.

•

By invention and dexterity everything may be delineated gracefully on paper, either in writing or painting.

•

Poetry is only an active, productive use of our powers; thought is the same. Hence poetry and thought may be identical, for in thought the senses reproduce their accumulated impressions, transmuted into a fresh form, from which fresh ideas take their rise.

•

All purely comic characters must, as in the old plays, be roughly, broadly, sketched in; fine distinctions are prosaic. In the region of poetry, every touch must be incisive, every action full of animation and colour.

•

No one should attempt to portray anything which he is not completely acquainted with and understands clearly.

•

There is a similarity with a difference between Erasmus, Ligne, and Voltaire. Jacobi also belongs to the transcendental empiricists. An empiricist is a passive thinker who deduces his facts from experience. Voltaire and almost all French philosophers are pure empiricists. Ligne has a tendency to transcendentalism. There is an easy transition thence to dogmatism; the next evolution produces enthusiasts and transcendentalists – then Kant, Fichte, and idealism.

•

*Meister* is not rich in descriptions of natural scenery. Goethe seldom touches upon landscape. Once, in the fourth part, before the attack by robbers, Goethe alludes to the romantic ridge of hills; but he does not concern himself much with the outer world.

•

There is a never-ceasing variety of conversation, description, and reflection in *Meister*. Conversation takes the larger share. There is less of reflection.

Story and reflection are interwoven, in the same way as conversation and description. Descriptions of character alternate with action. The theme is never hurried; edicts and opinions are carried out to a logical conclusion. The peculiarities of a novel affect the style. Both philosophy and morality are romantic. The smallest circumstances, as well as the most important, are treated with romantic irony. The leading points are not logical, but metrical and melodious, giving rise to that wonderful, romantic arrangement which pays no heed to rank or merit, high or low, superiority or inferiority. All the epithets are marvellously well chosen, with a true poetic discrimination. In the first book, we see how common, everyday incidents interest by the way in which they are put before us. Just in the same manner one may preserve a charming recollection of a quiet afternoon spent with people obsessed of no great talent, but who, by the harmony of their surroundings, and their bright, well-ordered lives, diffuse peace and happiness around them.

•

When we attentively consider the Laocoon, it may occur to us that there was a higher ideal than the ancients could grasp. Not that of wild defiance, but of resistance passing into resignation. Should not the sculptor always seize the moment of repose, and only that, for his art?

•

Fables with morals tacked on are like pictures underneath which the draughtsman explains what he meant to portray. Lessing often gives us an epigram in a fable – there it is welcome.

• Is not music an analytical combination, and *vice versa*. The harmony of numbers and acoustics belong to analytical combination. Numbers are mathematical vowels; all numbers are numerators. Analytical combination leads to the art of composition by numbers, as in thoroughbass. Speech is a musical instrument; the poet, orator, and philosopher play and compose by rules of grammar. A fugue is embodied logic or science; it can also be treated poetically. Thoroughbass is musical algebra and analysis. Analytical combination is critical algebra and analysis, and musical composition is to thoroughbass what analytical combination is to simple analysis. Many mathematical problems can only be solved in combination with others – from a higher point of view.

•

In Shakespeare there is a constant interchange of poetry and anti-poetry, harmony and discord, the low and common with the elevated and beautiful truth and fancy, the real and the imaginary; in this he is a perfect contrast to the Greeks.

•

Shakespeare's works and poems resemble the prose of Boccaccio and Cervantes, thoroughly elegant, crisp, and complete.

•

*Hans Sachs* is a sketch of a peculiar, allegorical, truly German mythology.

•

The poet's realm is the world compressed into the focus of his own times. He can make use of any topic, only he must do so with spirit. He must set forth both commonplace and extraordinary events; all effects are produced by contrast, and he is absolutely free to use whatever material he likes. Lifeless descriptions offer no interest; they do not touch either heart or soul; they must at least be symbolical, like nature herself, if they do not excite the deepest emotions. Above all, the poet must be no egotist. He is the representative prophet of nature, as the philosopher is the natural prophet of imagination. To the one all is objective, to the other all is subjective. The one is the voice of creation, the other the voice of the simple unit; one is song, the other talk.

•

The poet is ever true. He remains faithful to nature, and her recurrent cycles. All the poet's delineations must be symbolical or emotional. The symbolical does not touch the feelings at once, but it gives rise to spontaneous action. The one excites and rouses, the other touches and moves; the one affects the intellect, the other appeals to natural feeling; the one leads from appearances to actuality, the other from actuality to appearance. Formerly the poet could be all things to all men; life's circle was so narrow, and men's experience, knowledge, customs, and character so much alike, their requirements so much simpler.

•

An aesthetic work must be systematic and modified so as to be a complete whole. Even in the most humorous books, Wieland, Richter, and most comic writers fail in this. There is a superfluity of irrelevant and wearisome matter, as *hors d'œuvres* in their works. It is very rare to find the plan and the distribution of the plot carried out aesthetically. They have only aesthetic humour, not real comical feeling and wit.

•

Schiller draws too clearly and sharply to appear true to the eye; like Albert Dürer, not like Titian; too ideal in fact to seem natural.

•

We bear the sins of our fathers as we inherit their virtues: thus men live ever in the past and the future, and never less than in the present.

•

Weariness is mental hunger.

•

Children are antiques. Youth also. But not all youths are youthful. Grown-up persons are relatively young. Children are *terra incognita*.

•

Man is always alone, even with those he loves best.

•

The craving for love denotes that our nature is incomplete and weak.

•

Marriage is the greatest of all mysteries. It is a pity that there is no medium between loneliness and marriage. They are extremes. How few are capable of enduring solitude; how few have the right gifts for happy union. There are unions of all kinds, but true marriage is eternal.

•

Water contains all the elements of health; it is a joy even to touch it.

•

Gambling is tying experiments with chance.

•

Discontent, and many other faults, arise from want of power.

•

I can do what I will. Nothing is impossible to man.

•

Thought is a muscular action.

•

The antithesis between body and soul is one of the most remarkable and dangerous kind. This opposition plays a great role in history.

•

The historian must often make oratorical statements. He has a gospel to deliver – all history is a gospel.

•

The one great charm of a republic is that everything is unrestrained. Virtues, vices, good and evil, wisdom and folly, talent and stupidity, are all seen in the strongest light. Thus a republic resembles a tropical climate.

•

Health, comfort, and content are personal feelings, and depend only indirectly on external circumstances. Hence, perhaps, the source of mythological personifications.

•

He who has no feeling for religion – still has some rule of

conduct which takes its place. This causes much confusion, as he uses the same terms, only with different meanings.

•

Religion cannot be taught otherwise than love and patriotism. If one wished to make anyone in love, how would one accomplish it?

•

Every unjust action and unworthy thought is a treachery to love.

•

What a strange, incomprehensible hieroglyphic is man! How hard it is to understand him. There is much that is false in the belief that the outward corresponds with the inward man. Very ugly men have beautiful souls. Occasionally the hieroglyphic has moments of revelation.

•

History is one great anecdote. An anecdote is an historical molecule or epigram. Voltaire has written history by anecdotes – a most interesting work of art. The general form of history is a fusion of anecdotes. An artist must know how to turn every occurrence into anecdote. Anecdotes are like a gallery of humanity, showing the characteristics of mankind. A genuine anecdote is poetic. It satisfies the imagination.

•

The most wonderful and eternal phenomenon is oneself. Man is the greatest of mysteries. The history of the world is the answer to this problem. Philosophy, science, and literature all seek to solve the riddle. Its attraction will never cease as long as men exist.

•

Dreams have a high degree of interest to the psychologist, also to the historian of humanity. Dreams have largely contributed to the culture and education of men – hence the great importance formerly attached to them.

•

Woman is the symbol of beauty and goodness; man, of truth

and law.

•

We are united by closer bonds with the unseen, than with the seen.

•

The synthesis of body and soul is called person; the person is to the spirit what the body is to the soul. It fades away, but arises in a nobler form.

•

Commerce is the moving spirit of the world. It sets everything in motion, and unites everything, arouses countries and towns, nations and the arts, and is the spirit of culture, the perfection of human society.

•

The simplification and combination of science, and the transformation of all sciences into one, is an exercise for philosophy, which the love of science demands.

•

As disease is so rife among mankind, and each individual has so much to struggle against, it must be a very important element in life. As yet we do not know how best to make use of this element. Apparently it is a strong stimulant to reflection and action. In this field a rich harvest may be garnered, especially as regards the intellect, and in the department of morals, religion, and God knows in what other points also. Suppose I become the prophet of this new art.

•

There is much that is local and temporary in the *Old Testament*. The *Gospel* lays the foundation of future and nobler gospels.

•

The individual soul must be brought into harmony with the soul of the universe.

•

Light in action; light is like life – a force; light makes fire – it is the genius of the fire.

❖ 176

•

With the ancients, religion certainly was what it ought to be with us – poetry.

•

A blooming country is a more royal work than a park. Tasteful parks are an English invention. It ought to be a German invention, to have such a country as satisfies all the best aspirations of heart and intellect! He who could accomplish that would be the king of inventors.

•

A truly royal couple would be to mankind what a constitution is to the understanding. What is law, unless it is the expression of the will of a beloved and revered being?

•

Mystic sovereignty, like all ideas, requires a symbol. What symbol is more suitable than a lovable and an excellent man? Condensed definitions are much prized; and is not a perfect man a more beautiful symbol of a spirit than all the arguments of a learned College? He who is gifted with a great mind cares little for barriers and distinctions. Only small minds feel restrictions. A born king is better than an elected one. The best of men cannot endure elevation with impunity. He who is a born king is neither dazzled nor over-excited by his position. After all, is not the birthright the earliest of all? He can have thought but little who does not perceive its tendency to concord.

•

Whoever approaches this subject from historical ground has no idea what I mean, and from what point of view I am considering things. I speak Arabic to him, and he had best go his way, and not mix himself up with hearers whose idiom and customs are absolutely strange to him.

•

Most revolutionary leaders did not know what they were aiming at – form or deformity.

•

Revolutions are no proof of real energy in a nation. There is an energy arising from weakness which is often more forcible than true energy, but ends in greater weakness.

•

When one passes judgment on a nation, one is only judging the elements which are on the surface.

•

Is there any real difference between the temporal and the spiritual? Or is this a legacy from *Old Testament* days. Judaism is directly opposed to Christianity, but is the foundation of all theology.

•

The Gothic is the most truly religious church architecture.

•

A philosopher lives on problems, as an ordinary human being does on food. An insoluble problem is very indigestible food. What spice is to food, such is a paradox to a problem. A problem is only solved when it is annihilated. So also with food. The profit derived from both is increased activity. In philosophy my intelligence is not only exercised, but improved; which is only true of food to a certain extent. A sudden increase of intelligence is as doubtful as a sudden increase of strength. All true progression in health and intellect is slow; though this varies according to temperament. No one eats to acquire a new development; still less does one philosophize to find new truths. One philosophizes because one lives. If one could attain such a point as to live without food, one might philosophize without fixed problems.

•

Some men have far-stretching views; others more temporary ones. Can this cause the difference between heroes and artists?

•

All that is good in the world is the immediate work of God. One can see God in every man. There is an eternity of thought in Christianity. The more one studies it, the grander, and vaster, and more glorious it seems.

•

Schelling's natural philosophy presents a narrow view of nature and philosophy. Schelling is the philosopher of the new chemistry.

•

What are slaves? – repressed and weakened men. What are Sultans? – slaves over-excited by luxury. What is the tendency of both? – violence and madness. How can slaves be cured? – by careful emancipation and enlightenment: they must be treated like frost-bitten men. Sultans? – as Dionysius and Crœsus: by terror, fasting, and conventual discipline, gradually employing mental restoratives. Sultans and slaves are the extremes. There are many intermediate classes, from the king to the true cynic. Bullies and sycophants belong to the classes next to Sultans and slaves, and, like these, are interchangeable. Both are represent-ative forms of weakness.

•

All attractions are relative, except one, which is absolute.

•

The most complete temperaments are formed by complete union with this attraction. It is so powerful that with it one requires no other, and becomes utterly indifferent to all others. This attraction is perfect love.

•

Too much excitability and sensibility shows a want of capacity – as one sees in fantastic enthusiasts.

•

Death is the romantic principle of our lives. Death is the cross of life. Through death, life becomes strong.

•

One must learn to look on the world as one great property, and study its economy.

•

Governments must learn at last that they can only attain their objects by working in common.

•

There is no higher enjoyment than in learning; and the feeling of power is the source of all pleasure.

•

What attracts most is the unknown. The well known has no further attraction. The power of perception is in itself the greatest of charms.

•

Nothing is so great a preservative against folly as activity and technical work.

•

Real enjoyment is a *perpetuum mobile*; it is ever reproducing itself. The cessation of this activity is the cause of all the discontent and dissatisfaction in the world.

•

Why is there no mastery in religion? Because it is founded on love. Schleiermacher was the prophet of an art religion – much such a worship as artists bestow on the ideal and the beautiful. Love is free, and chooses as dearest the poorest and the neediest. God loves the poor and the sinner. A loveless nature is irreligious. Religious problem: Sympathy with the Godhead gives rise to pity. If we are to love God, must we not feel He calls for our sympathy? How far has Christianity answered this problem?

•

The life of a cultivated man should alternate between music and silence, as between day and night.

•

Christianity is an historical religion permeated by morality and poetry.

•

Intellect, soul, earnestness, and knowledge are inextricably associated with Divine things.

•

Fascination is a kind of artistic madness. All passion is a kind of spell. A fascinating girl is more truly an enchantress than people think.

•

It seems quite natural to confide in doctors and clergymen, for all who come in contact with them know that they alone can help in certain crises of life.

•

Only he who is independent of society is real good company. Society must not attract me, if I wish to be its attraction. It must seek and desire my presence, and I must be able to take the prevailing tone; a gift which is called tact. I must allow myself to give pleasure to others and share my thoughts with them.

•

Scepticism is often immature idealism. The idealist who does not understand himself is a realist.

•

The heart is the key to the world and to life. The helplessness of man's position leads him to love and be bound to others. The very imperfection of his nature makes him sensitive to the influence of others. In illness we are dependent on our fellowcreatures; and this feeling of mutual sympathy is one object of life. From this point of view, Christ was the key to the world.

•

Any sudden rupture of love or friendship is like a shipwreck.

•

As earthly beings, we strive to obtain spiritual perfection, especially intellectual development; as spiritual beings, we strive for earthly cultivation and bodily perfection. These two objects can only be attained by morality.

•

A demon who could appear, really appear, to men, must be a good spirit; a man who could work miracles, and be in affinity with the spirit-world, must also be good. A man who can become a spirit is at the same time a spirit who could become man.

•

Sensuality is to love what sleep is compared to life.

•

The more occupations a man has, provided they are not disturbing and clashing, the more energy he has for thought.

•

Selfishness is the source of all abasement; self-diffusion the basis of all elevation. The first step is to look inward. He who stops at that has achieved but little. The second step is to look outward with a penetrating, reflective glance. No one can ever describe anything well who can only chronicle his own experiences and sensations. He must be able to throw himself into the experiences of others, and this requires both diligence and leisure. The true author must be able to describe everything. This gives a free style such as one admires in Goethe.

•

In most religious systems we are considered members of the Godhead; members which, if they will not obey the impulsion of the guiding will, but will follow their own instincts, and refuse the rights of membership – have to submit to surgical treatment, and either be painfully cured or cut off.

•

Love is the goal of the world's history – the Amen of the universe.

•

What is really old? What is young? Young when the future preponderates; old when remembrance is the chief factor.

•

The more quietly and slowly one begins, the greater perfection one can attain. The more one can do with little, so much the more one can do with much. When one loves one person, one has learnt how best to love all mankind.

•

To overcome temptation is more praiseworthy than to avoid it.

•

Nothing is more singular in religion than the new idea promulgated by Christianity of a common humanity and a universal religion. From thence arose proselytism. Strange, too, the scattering of the Jews, and the spread of the new teaching among a civilized and conquering nation, which transmitted it to rude and conquered tribes.

•

Carbon and diamonds are the same in substance – and yet how different! May not man and woman bear the same comparison? We are clay, and women are the rubies and sapphires, which are equally products of clay.

•

Religion alone really unites men.

• The preacher must seek first of all to arouse enthusiasm, for this is the element of religion. Every word must be clear, warm, and hearty. He must seek to separate his flock from the world, and give them *esprit de corps* to enable them to rise to a higher scale of life, ennoble their practice, and fill them with high aspirations.

•

Most of Lavater's hymns are too earthly: too much morality and asceticism; too little actuality, too little mysticism. Hymns must be much more animated, fervent, popular, and yet mystic. Sermons ought not to be dogmatic, but of a nature to excite the holiest devotion and to animate the heart. Sermons and hymns may treat of stories. Tales have a very religious effect. Instruction and moral sermons belong to a different category. Sermons must be inspirations and revelations. Repose, architecture, music, and ritual all tend to impress the congregation. True religion expresses itself in pure, life-stirring enthusiasm, which elevates everything. Both hymns and sermons must be simple.

•

He who seeks God will find Him everywhere.

•

Every reflecting man will seek out truth, and find it whatever he does, wherever he goes.

•

No one need expect justice in this world.

•

Science is only one half; faith is the completion.

•

Fortune and misfortune are both negative and positive.

•

Poetry permeates us with the individuality of another.

•

Nature has allegories of her own. The mists rising from the waters are like prayer.

# MORE FUGITIVE THOUGHTS

We are near awakening when we dream that we dream.

•

All that is good in the world is the immediate action of God. God can be manifested to me in any human being. It requires an eternity to comprehend Christianity. The more one studies it the higher and more manifold are its glories.

•

The best of the French monarchs longed that every one of his subjects could be rich enough to have a fowl for his Sunday dinner. Would not that be a still better government which made the peasant prefer bread and cheese in his own land to dainties elsewhere; and which excited him to thank God daily for having cast his lot in so favoured a land. This is the age of the letter – not the spirit. It is not much to the honour of the age that it is so opposed to nature, so indifferent to family life, so disinclined to the highest, most poetic form of society. Who will be more amazed than our Cosmopolitan when the era of eternal peace arises, and the highest development of which human nature is capable is presented to him in the form of a monarch? The worthless cement which now binds communities will crumble into dust, and the spirit will drive away the ghosts which have taken his place, pens, paper, and printing-presses which have dismembered him – then all mankind will love each other like two betrothed.

•

The King is the principle of life in the State; as the sun is to the planets. Next to the life principle is the highest life, the atmosphere of light. Every citizen is more or less affected by it. In the presence of the King every utterance becomes brilliant, poetic, and full of animation. The more animated the spirit is, the greater is its energy; the energy produces reflection, and animated thought is the perfection of reflection – even so the utterances of the citizens in their monarch's presence are the expressions of the highest activity of the intellect, tempered by self-restraint and subordination to rule! No Court can exist without etiquette. There is a natural etiquette, noble and beautiful – an artificial etiquette, stilted and distasteful. The restoration of the first will be no unimportant part of the monarch's care, as it will have a profound influence on the appreciation and love of monarchy.

•

A Republic is the *Fluidum deferns* of youth. Where there are young people – there is a Republic.

•

Marriage alters the system. The married man longs for order, security, and peace; he seeks to establish a real family life – a genuine monarchy.

•

A Prince with no family feelings is no monarch.

•

Would not that be absolute monarchy? To what arbitrary power would one not be exposed?

•

In all circumstances is not the individual exposed to arbitrary rule? – even if I went into a desert, would not my real interest be the arbitrary rule of my individuality? Is not each person ruled by his own character? In a perfect democracy, I am swayed by many; in a representative democracy by fewer; under a monarchy, by one arbitrary power.

•

Does not reason claim that every man should be his own lawgiver? A man will only obey his own laws.

•

Whence did Solon and Lycurgus derive such true and universal laws? – Probably from their experience and self-knowledge. If I am a man like them, whence do I derive my laws? From the same source – and if I live according to the laws of Solon and Lycurgus, am I faithless to reason? Every true law is my law, whoever enacts it. This process of evolving laws cannot be easy, or else we should not need written laws. It is not a science in itself. A long and weary apprenticeship is obligatory on the judge. Whence arise guilds and states? – from want of time and power in the individual. Every human being cannot learn and practise every science and art. Labour and arts are divided. Is not government on the same footing? If all are capable of achieving all, why is not every man a doctor, a poet, and so on. The impossibility of this is conceded in all other branches except philosophy and statesmanship – every one believes himself capable of criticizing these, and assumes the right to lay down the law like a virtuoso.

•

The excellence of representative Democracy is undeniable. A natural, exemplary man is a poet's dream. Consequently it is needful to construct one artificially. The best men complete one another. Association arouses a pure spirit of community. Their decrees are emanations – the idealized government is realised.

•

But I doubt this community of feeling among the best of men. I will not appeal even to common experience. It is obvious that no living body can rise from dead matter – no just, unselfish, liberal men can come together from a mass of useless, unjust, selfish beings. It will be long before people realize this simple truth, and see that a one-sided majority will be partial. Such a majority will not elect the most excellent men; on the contrary, it will admire mediocrity and mere worldly wisdom. By mediocrity I mean those whose nature is toned down to the commonplace, the classic model of the masses. The worldly wise are the courtiers of the masses. This will develop no high spirit, still less extreme purity; a great mechanism will be built up, swayed by intrigue. The reins of government will waver between devotion to the letter and manifold party influences. The despotism of one is preferable to the despotism of the many, as it saves time and shoe-leather, when one knows where the ruling power is, and it shows its cards; while in the rule of the majority you know not in what hole or corner the power is hidden, or what means to take to ingratiate yourself with it.

•

If the representative becomes riper and purer on account of the eminence to which he is raised, why do not the same causes affect the sole ruler? If mankind was what it ought to be and should be, all forms of government would be indifferent, for men would everywhere be governed by universal laws. In that case the first thing they would do would be to choose the most beautiful, poetic, and most natural form – the family form – monarchy. Many masters, many families; one master, one family.

•

The Hernhüter (Moravians) strive to influence and lead children's minds. But is this the best thing? Is it not grandmotherly – old woman's management? When Christ says, "Except ye become as little children," he means unsophisticated children, not spoilt, effeminate, modern children.

•

What is more than life? Life service, the service of light.

•

The first man was the first spirit seer; all appears to him as spirit. What are children but first men? The fresh gaze of the child is richer in significance than the forecasting of the most undoubted seer.

•

It is only because we are weak and self-conscious, that we do not realize that in life is Fairyland. All fairy tales are mere dreams of the home world, which is everywhere and nowhere. Our higher powers which one day, like the genii, shall carry out all our wishes, are for the present merely Muses, which refresh us on our weary path with the charm of memory.

·

Man's life is truth. If he boldly confesses truth, he confesses himself. If he denies truth, he betrays his nature. We speak not here of lies, but of acting against conviction.

·

Properly speaking, there is no such thing as misfortune. Happiness and misfortune stand in continual balance. Every misfortune is, as it were, the obstruction of a stream, which, after overcoming the obstacle, bursts through with the greater energy.

·

The ideal of morality has no more dangerous rival than the ideal of strength and power, which has been falsely named the poetic ideal. It is only the ideal of a savage, though in these days it has gained many adherents among the effeminate. This ideal reduces man to a beast-spirit, whose brutal power influences the weak by a brutal attraction.

·

The spirit of Poetry is like the dawn, which draws music from the statue of Memnon.

·

The *Bible* begins nobly with Paradise, the symbol of youth; and concludes with the Eternal Kingdom, the Holy City. Its two main divisions are genuine grand historical divisions. Each portion contains a magnificent subject symbolically treated. The beginning of the *New Testament* is the second Atonement, the inauguration of the New Era. Every man's history should be a living *Bible*. Christ is a new Adam. A *Bible* is the crucial test of authorship.

·

As yet there is no religion. There must be a school for genuine religion. Think ye that religion exists! It has to be made and carried out into practice by the sympathetic union of men.

•

There are many ways by which we may make ourselves independent of materiality. Firstly, by blunting our senses – by custom, exhaustion, or insensibility; secondly, by moderation, useful employment, and alternative influences – which are remedies; thirdly, by maxims (a) of contempt, (b) and hatred to all emotions. The Stoics and the savages of North America *despise* outer influences. Anchorites, monks, fakirs, and penitents in all ages adopted the principle of hatred to the material. Many criminals and evil doers have partially adhered to this. Both maxims fuse into one another. There is a fourth way, by the nature being raised by a higher attraction far above the influence of lower attractions, and set entirely free from their power. Passions of all kinds, faith and confidence in ourselves or another, belief in ghosts, deliver men from the thraldom of actuality. Opinions and judgments claim equally to be free. Thus we can become utterly independent of the world of sense, and grow more and more attached to the world of symbol, seeing no charm save in it. This often occurs to learned men, who take little pleasure in the absolute and inevitable decrees of sense.

•

On the other hand, one finds people who hate all symbolism, and will not hear of it; these are rough-souled folk, who repudiate all such knowledge for themselves, and whose idle, coarse, slavish views have been embodied in a system by Rousseau, Helvetius, Locke, & c. – a system which has gained much ground in our day.

•

A rupture of love or friendship is a shipwreck.

•

Every man has his individual mode of expression. Speech is a spirit utterance. Genuine utterances give rise to clear ideas. As soon as a thing is rightly named one has a clear comprehension of it.

• One cannot but shrink in alarm when one considers the power of spirit. There is no limit to will and thought. In this way it resembles heaven. The power of imagination flags in all efforts to comprehend it. It leads us to comprehend mental diseases, mental weakness; and the moral law shines forth as the only true system of life-development – the ground-work of harmonious progress. Mankind advances by slow stages, but every successive stage is easier, and marks a true growth.

•

The historian learns his craft from newspapers and contemporary writings. He learns from these how to criticize. He learns to discriminate one-sided and false accounts. Perfectly contrasting testimonies neutralize one another. Incomplete accounts give a truthful result, when analyzed and corrected by each other. Newspapers and histories are the sources from which the historian draws his information. Time is the great historian.

•

What is actually young? what old? Young when the future preponderates; old, when the past sways the mind.

•

When you see a giant look at the position of the sun; it may be that it is but the shadow of a pigmy.

•

May not the devil, as father of lies, be only a necessary ghost? Deception and illusion are opposed to truth, virtue, and religion. Caprice, superstition, slavish fatalism, bad tempers, and perversity are opposed to free will.

•

Where there are no gods ghosts bear sway.

•

Martyrs are spiritual heroes. Every man passes through his martyr years. Christ was the great martyr of our race; He hallowed martyrdom.

•

Prayer is to religion what thought is to philosophy. Prayer is making religion, sermons should be players. Religion has its own world, its peculiar element.

• 

The Holy Spirit is more than the *Bible*; He should be our teacher, not the dead, earthly, ambiguous letter.

• 

It is strange how our sacred history resembles a fairy tale. It commences with an evil spell, which is overcome by a marvellous expiation, and the spell is broken.

• 

The man of letters is the instinctive enemy of sacerdotalism: the literary and the clerical class must wage a war of extermination when they disagree, for both aim at the same position. The division between them became more sharply accentuated after the Reformation, especially in recent years, when Europe in manhood approached the epoch of triumphant learning; knowledge and faith then assumed an antagonistic attitude. To the generally prevailing faith was attributed the universal degradation, which it was fondly hoped would be overcome by increasing knowledge. Religious feeling was attacked on all sides, both as to its present condition and ancient form. This result of modern thought was named Philosophy, and in this was included all that opposed old lines of thought, and consequently all that opposed itself to religion. The original personal hatred to the Catholic faith passed into hatred of the *Bible*, the Christian faith, and at last against all religion. Nay, more, this hatred of religion naturally extended to all objects of enthusiasm in general; fancy and feeling, morality and love of art, the future and the past, were alike proscribed; man was placed in the front rank of creation; and the eternal, creative music of the universe was changed to the monotonous chatter of a gigantic mill, which, turned by the stream of chance, and floating thereon, was a mill of itself, without architect and miller, properly a genuine *perpetuum mobile,* a real self-grinding mill.

Only one enthusiasm was generously granted to poor Humanity, and made a touchstone of highest culture for all dabblers in the same: enthusiasm for this lordly and high and mighty Philosophy; above all, for its priests and mystagogues. France was so happy as to be the cradle and seat of this new faith, which had been patched up out of scraps of pure knowledge. Much as poetry was despised in this new Church, still there were some poets among them, who, for the sake of effect, used the old ornaments and the old lights, though in so doing the new system ran a risk of being consumed by ancient fire. Lest enthusiasm should become contagious, there were always worldly-wise members of the community at hand to extinguish so perilous a condition with a flood of icy water. The chief object of the community was to purge all science, nature, the universe, and the human soul from all taint of poetry, to obliterate all vestige of the holy, disgust people with all that was noble and elevated, by scathing sarcasm, and thus rob life of all beauty. In Germany they set about the same business in a more thorough way; education was reformed, a new, commonplace form was given to religion, all that was marvellous and mysterious being carefully shunted. Even history ceased to be a refuge for the intellectual, as it was reduced to a family picture of the household burgher life; God was reduced to the role of an idle spectator of men's fine deeds, which received due meed of praise only from the pen of some poet or playwright. Sad to say, Nature continued as wondrous and mysterious, as poetical and infinite as ever, in spite of these well-meant endeavours to modernize her! If by chance any old superstition of a higher world and such like came to the surface, instantly all the rattles were sprung, that the dangerous spark might be extinguished at once by philosophy and sarcasm. Yet, strange to say, tolerance was the watchword of the learned, and in France it was synonymous with philosophy. This history of modern belief is highly remarkable, and offers the key to all the vast phenomena of recent times. Not till the last century, till the latter half does this novelty arise; and in a short time it spread to monstrous bulk and variety. A second Reformation, more comprehensive and specific, was unavoidable; and it naturally first visited that country which was most modernized, and had longest lain in an exhausted condition, from want of freedom. Now, however, we stand on an eminence, and look down with friendly smile on those bygone days, discerning curious historical crystallisations even in such marvellous follies. Thankfully do we stretch out our hands to these men of letters and philosophers for this illusion had to be exhausted, so that true science might gain her rightful place. Poetry arises, like a leafy India, more beauteous and many hued, in contrast with the icy, dead Spitzbergen of that armchair philosophy. To produce a glorious, luxuriant India requires vast expanses of cold, motionless sea, barren cliffs, the starry heavens veiled by mist, long nights, and frozen Poles. The deep meaning of the laws of mechanism lay heavy on those anchorites in the deserts of understanding; the charm of the first glance into it over-powered them: the old avenged itself on them; to the first breath of that new ideal they sacrificed all that the world held fairest and holiest. They were the first to practise and preach the sacredness of Nature, the infinitude of Art, the independence of knowledge, the all-presence of the spirit of History; and so doing, they ended a spectre dynasty more powerful and terrific than perhaps even they were aware of.

# THOUGHTS ON PHILOSOPHY
# AND PHYSICS

Everything that one thinks – thinks out originally – is a thought-problem.

•

Abstract words are among other words like gas – invisible.

•

That alone is spiritual which ceaselessly reveals itself to the spirit; often assuming new and varied forms. Not merely once at the outset, as in so many philosophical systems.

•

Where a genuine faculty for reflection rules the mind, there is progress. Many learned men have not this faculty. They have learned induction and deduction as a cobbler learns to make shoes, and it never occurred to them to find out the originating cause of thoughts. But then no other way is to be trusted. Many people have a love of reflection only for a time. It increases or diminishes with advancing years, or by the discovery of some system or method, which appears to save them the trouble of further thought.

•

The highest task of culture is self-mastery of the inner life, so that it may indeed be the true I, *ego*. Without complete selfknowledge one can never understand others.

•

All is chaos and confusion without abstraction, but afterwards chaos is metamorphosed into a union of independent beings – a crowd has become an orderly community.

•

Experience is the touchstone of reason, and vice-versa. Practical people often remark on the insufficiency of theories in practical matters, while philosophers, on their side, observe the difficulty of theorizing on experience. The practical man casts theory away, not reflecting on the problematic answer to this question, Does theory exist for practice, or. practice for theory? The narrower a system is, the more it pleases the worldly-wise. Thus the materialistic; teaching, the systems of Helvetius and Locke, were loudly applauded by this class. In the same way, Kant has now a larger following than Fichte.

•

In the early days of the inquiry into the judgment every new opinion was a discovery. The value of the opinion increased according to the application which could be made of it. Aphorisms, which seem to us now mere commonplaces, belonged then to a higher grade of intellectual life. One must have both genius and penetration to discover the relative value of new statements. Keen observation on the peculiarities of mankind, whether in ordinary or unusual positions, necessarily excites the deepest interest in all who think. Thus apothegms arose, which have been valued at all times, among all nations. It is quite probable that future ages may in like manner look down on our most prized discoveries. The restless spirit of mankind, ever occupied with newer and higher problems, may class our cherished theories with the commonplace proverbs of the past. • Fichte and Kant have achieved a systematic method.

•

Fichte's adoption of a universal prevailing thought is the keystone of his philosophy. Logic is the result of knowledge. Philosophy begins with ephemeral thought; it takes its rise like a breath.

• Theoretical science proves the reality of logic, its connection with the rest of nature, and its conformity to mathematics, its capabilities in the way of discovery and accuracy. The mind is the power which judges, discriminates, and sanctions. The member of speech is the cleverest, and thinks itself so to be; the same can be said of the mind.

•

Zeal for knowledge is wonderfully compounded out of love of knowledge and desire to penetrate the unknown.

•

Logic is the grammar of the highest speech-thought. It consists only in the definition of ideas, the mechanism of thought, the pure physiology of ideas. Logical ideas bear the same relation to one another as words without thoughts. Logic concerns itself only with the inanimate bodies of thoughts. Metaphysics are the dynamics of thought; they teach the origin of the power of thought, and are occupied with the spirit of logic. Men often wonder at the incompleteness of both these sciences; how each stands, as it were, alone, and has no community with the other. From the earliest ages a union between them was attempted, but it always failed, for one or the other lost its distinctive character. They remained metaphysical logic and logical metaphysics, but neither were satisfactory.

•

Physiology and psychology, mechanics and chemistry, fared no better. Towards the end of this century there arose great excitement about this; everything seemed in a state of ferment-ation, followed by terrific explosions. Many asserted that old barriers had been overthrown, and that a principle of union and eternal peace was growing and spreading in all directions, so that soon there would be but one science and one mind – even as there was one Prophet and one God.

•

Schoolmen are crude, discursive thinkers. The true scholar is a subtle mystic, who builds up his universe with logical atoms; he annihilates nature, and replaces it with an artificial thought world. His goal is a perfect automaton.

●

The poet is his antipodes; he hates rules and systems. Nature is to him the embodiment of wild, powerful life; animation abounds; there is no law, all is miracle and impulse. He is purely dynamic.

●

Thus the spirit of philosophy takes its rise in two perfectly opposed forms.

• In the second stage of culture these forms approximate; as the union of extremes gives rise to means, so from this approximation arises eclecticism and endless confusion. At this stage the narrowest views seem the most important; pure philosophy takes a lower place. The actual and present seem the boundaries of thought. The philosophers of the first class look down with contempt on those of the second class; they call their observations incomplete, their views weak and illogical. These return the compliment, and look down on their opponents as absurd enthusiasts. From the latter set arise scholastics and alchemists, from the former thinkers; the former have genius, the latter talent. These have ideas, those plans; on one side are heads without hands, on the other, hands without heads.

●

The artist who unites both genius and power of work reaches a third stage. He has both power to think and to act; he sees that both principles harmonize. This is the commencement of true spiritual life, which never ends.

●

Sophists are those who are ever on the watch for the faults and weaknesses of philosophers, and draw deductions from them to their own advantage. They have nothing in common with philosophy, and must be looked upon as enemies, and treated as such. The most dangerous among them are the sceptics, who hate philosophy. Ordinary sceptics are very commendable people.

•

They have a genuinely philosophic gift of criticism, but are wanting in mind power. They are dissatisfied with existing systems; not one seems able to *vitalize* them; they have genuine taste, but not the energy of production. They are mere controversialists. All eclectics are sceptics; the more they study, the more sceptical they become. A proof of this is that the greatest and best of scientific men have always at the end of their lives confessed how little they know.

•

The duty of philosophy is to animate and vivify. Formerly philosophy was first killed, then dissected and analysed. Philosophy was put in the category of *caput mortuum*. All attempts at reconstruction failed. It is only of late years that philosophy has been considered a living science; and it may actually come about that new philosophies may be called into existence.

•

The criterion of its logical usefulness is its power of applicability. There are logical Philistines and logical artists. Another criterion of art is in its power of expression, which is a gift philosophy must acquire. One critic lays down this axiom: philosophy must contain nothing opposed to conventionality, and must agree with the prevailing manners, opinions, and religion. Such an axiom demands that philosophy should never pass the barriers of material proof; it must not make common cause with poetry; it must not be *à la portée* of the common crowd; but have a language of its own, pertaining to the lecture-room. No, says another, it must be amusing; at home with the peasant and the artizan, adaptable to all circumstances; it must have nothing to do with religion, and may shrug its shoulders at the moralists; it must understand about everything, and so on. Thus, every one stamps it with the dearest wish of his heart, and the demands of his own character, and one requires only to know a man's philosophy to understand him thoroughly. Many people change their philosophy as they do their servants and their wishes. At last they hate every kind of philosophy, and make a final choice. Now they think they have escaped from the demon, but they are more than ever in its grasp. Another class of easy-going, good-natured folks are preserved from these contests. They never venture to seize upon this Proteus, for they know nothing about him. The cleverest among them think that Proteus was the invention of idle brains: they have never seen him nor felt him, and deny his very existence, and thus become his humble subjects.

•

Self-sacrifice is a genuine philosophical act; this is the real commencement of all philosophy, to this tend all the efforts of the neophyte, and this alone is the sign of ideal life.

•

Philosophy is like all synthetic sciences, like mathematics – absolute. It is an ideal system of contemplating and regulating the inner life.

•

Fichte's method is the best proof of idealism. "What I will, I can." Nothing is impossible to man.

•

Philosophy is the science of self-analysis; the art of specifying, combining, and creating.

•

Analysis is divination, the art of discovery reduced to rules.

•

All ideas are related to one another: analogy means *air de famille*. By comparing several of the children of one family, one can divine the characteristics of the parents. All families arise from two causes, which are united, though of opposite different natures. Every family is the germ of endless individual forms of humanity.

•

By its very nature philosophy is anti-historical. It turns from the future to the practical; it is the science of perception; it explains the past by the future, whereas history takes the reverse process.

•

Synthetic thoughts are associated thoughts. As one reflects upon them, one is led to see the natural affinities and connection of thoughts. Thought should be at home in the realm of thought. The Socratic mind says philosophy is everywhere or nowhere, and that with a little trouble one can find out the drift of everything. The Socratic system seeks to discover truth under all conditions, and to ascertain the reciprocal conditions of various circumstances.

•

Philosophy is home-sickness, a longing everywhere to be at home.

•

All actual commencement is but secondary momentum. Everything which is seen involves a presupposition; its individual principle, its absolute self is precedent, must at any rate have been thought of first.

•

The commencement of the *ego* is ideal. It took its rise because it was preordained. The actual beginning is a later form – the beginning is subsequent to the *ego*, therefore the *ego* had no beginning. Here we are in the domain of art, but these scientific suppositions are the groundwork of a science founded on facts.

•

The *ego* = *non-ego* is the highest theme for science. In the same way criticism (both the exhaustive method and the inversion method) is the most fruitful of all philosophic teaching when brought to bear on ourselves, or the study of nature. We begin to perceive that nature or the outer world is similar to a human being; we find out that we can only begin to comprehend things in the same way in which we know ourselves and those dearest to us. At last we realize the true bond of union between subject and object, and discover that even in our own selves there is an outer world which stands in the same relation to our inner selves, that our outer life bears to the outer world; that the latter are as closely united as our own outer and inner life; therefore we can only comprehend the inner life and soul of nature by reflection, even as it is only by sensation that our outer life comes in contact with material forces.

•

Philosophy is the higher analogon of organism.

•

Organism is completed by philosophy, and inverted. They each symbolize the other.

•

True philosophy is realistic idealism or Spinozaism; it rests on the highest faith. Faith and idealism are inseparable.

•

Fichte's *non-ego* is a combination of all attractions, an eternal unknown. It is only life which attracts, and life cannot be enjoyed.

•

The difference between opinion and truth is obvious by their functions. Opinion arises from truth; truth is self-existent. Opinions can be eradicated like disease; opinion is only enthusiasm or Philistinism. The one leaves the mind exhausted, and it is only revived by a course of diminished excitement and stern self-control. The other leaves a deceptive animation, whose dangerous revolutionary symptoms can only be cured by increasing severity. Both dispositions of the mind require chronic and seriously conducted mental discipline.

•

Error and prejudice are burdens which excite independent minds to opposition, whereas they oppress weak minds.

•

A truthful description of error is an indirect definition of truth. True definition of truth is alone true. True definition of error is partly error; on the other side, a false description of error has truth in it.

•

To understand truth perfectly, one must polarize it. Falsehood, from the highest point of view, has a much worse side than the common acceptation. It builds up a false world, and is the cause of inextricable confusion. Falsehood is the source of all that is evil and bad.

•

The method of attaining truth must be much enlarged and simplified. One must seek to represent it everywhere and in everything.

•

There is no concrete philosophy. Philosophy is like the philosopher's stone, or the squaring of the circle, the ideal of science – the goal of the learned.

•

Fichte's teaching of science defines this ideal. Mathematics and physics are the only concrete sciences. Philosophy is intelligence itself. A perfect philosophy implies a perfect intellect.

•

The idea of philosophy is a mysterious tradition. Philosophy is an undefined science of science, the inciting, mystic spirit of science, incapable of being circumscribed in the definite limits of a special science. As all sciences are mutually interwoven, philosophy can never be limited or completed. Only when all other sciences are brought to perfection will philosophy be rightly understood.

•

We think of God as a person, as we think of ourselves as persons. God is just as personal and individual as we are, for our so-called *ego* is not our own *ego* but His reflection.

•

Some of our meditations have quite a distinct character from others. One feels as if engaged in converse with an unknown, enlightened being, who leads us in a wonderful way to solve the difficulties which oppress us. This being takes possession of our mind; it is a homogeneous being, for it treats man as a spiritual creature, and awakens his highest powers. This higher being bears the same relation to man that man does to nature, as the wise man to the child. Man longs to be like him, even as he tries to imitate the *non-ego*. This energizing spirit cannot be defined; each must realize it for himself. It is an energy of the highest nature, by which only the highest natures are impelled, but mankind is bound to strive to experience it.

•

Philosophizing is self-conversing, an opening out of the inner self, the arousing of the genuine *ego* by the idealistic *ego*. Philosophizing is the groundwork of all revelation; the determination to philosophize is the summons to the real *ego* to bestir itself, to awake, to be a spirit. Without philosophy there is no genuine morality; without morality, no philosophy.

•

All reflection on some particular object, or (which is the same thing) in one fixed direction, brings about a real connection with it; we realize the attraction it has for us, and the individual exertion which we have to make; not to lose the impression it produces on us, but to keep it steadily before us, so as to reach the goal of our desires.

•

Genuine collective philosophy is communion with a dearly loved world; a detachment from those advanced parts where there is the most antagonistic opposition to one's further progress. One follows the sun, and tears oneself from the place which, owing to the revolution of the planet, will be plunged for a time in cold night and mist. Death is a genuine act of philosophy.

•

In all systems of thought one particular idea or observation takes the lead and stifles all others. In the spiritual natural system one must seek them all around – each in its peculiar soil and climate – and give one's best care to produce a paradise of ideas. That is the genuine system. Paradise was the ideal of earthly life, and the question of its whereabouts is not unimportant. It has been scattered all over the world and has become unrecognizable.

Its scattered traits must be collected, its skeleton filled in. This is the regeneration of Paradise.

•

A man should work with all his energy at what seems difficult to him, until he can accomplish it with ease and dexterity. Then he loves what he has attained by hard work.

•

Transcendentalism is pure empiricism. The highest philosophy treats of the union of spirit and nature.

•

Philosophy cannot bake bread, but it can reveal God, freedom, and eternity.

•

Which, then, is most practical, philosophy or economy?

•

We only comprehend a subject so far as we can express it. The more easily and completely we can produce or define it, the better we understand it.

•

Description by tones and lines is an amazing abstraction.

•

Three letters are the sign of "God"; a few strokes conjure up millions of ideas. How amazingly concentrated are the symbols of the spirit-world! One word of command sets legions in motion; the word freedom rouses nations.

•

Contact with an object produces an effect which lasts as long as the contact lasts. That is the cause of all synthetic modifications of the individual.

•

There are one-sided and many-sided points of contact.

•

We are in connection with the whole universe, as with the future, so with the past. It depends upon ourselves entirely, on the direction we take and the perseverance we show, which of the various influences affect us most. Reduced to a system, this would be the long-sought art of discovery. Man is led by these laws, and it is indubitable that a searching course of self-observation would reveal them clearly.

•

Man arms himself with tools. One can say man could create a world if he had the needful apparatus for carrying out his ideas. The germ is in him. As the principle of a mighty war ship is conceived in the brain of the naval architect, and incorporated into actual existence by crowds of workmen and varied tools, even so a momentary thought gives rise to stupendous changes. In this way man is a creator.

•

How can a man have a wish to accomplish something unless he has the germ of it in his brain? There must be organic power first. Teaching merely develops and nourishes a pre-existing faculty.

•

Definitions are merely real or useless names. Ordinary names are merely marks.

•

Schemhamphorasch, the name of names.

•

A real definition is a magic word. Every idea has a scale of nomenclature, the highest, absolute, and incommunicable. Towards the middle of the scale they are commonplace, and end antithetically again in namelessness.

•

Abstraction is a withdrawal from the outer world. By analogy, earthly life would be abstraction for a spirit. Earthly life would thus arise from original reflection, self-abstraction as free as ours.

•

Contrariwise, spiritual life in this world arises from a breaking loose from ordinary reflections. The mind develops, rises above itself, and for the first time comprehends itself as *ego*.

•

By this we see what relative terms abstraction and expansion are. What we call abstraction is expansion.

•

All inwardly concentrated thought is, at the same time, an ascension, a view of the true outward.

•

We shall never understand ourselves perfectly; but we might do more than understand ourselves.

•

Ours is a mission. We are called to civilize the world. If a spirit appeared to us, we should be inspired by the conjunction of our spirit with his. There can be no revelation of a spirit without inspiration.

•

It is only because man remembers his origin that he can work in the realm of thought. Thought is the only spiritual influence in the world. Therefore it is a duty to think of the dead. It is the only way in which one can remain in communion with them. Is not God alone realized by faith?

•

A too great activity of the organs might be a dangerous gift in this earthly phase of existence. The spirit in its present condition might make a disturbing use of them. It is well that there is a certain dulness which hinders impulse, and which preserves the methodical joint action this earthly life requires.

•

The senses are tools and means.

•

All analogy is symbolical.

•

My body is complete in itself, and has a special individual principle which I call soul.

•

The animating principle of the soul seems inherent to it, and only indirectly influenced by the soul of the universe.

❖ 207

•

I can only experience anything in so far as I assimilate it with myself. It is an alienation of myself, an adoption of a new element into myself. The new product is different from the two original factors – a combination of both. I perceive that the change is twofold; the combination is mine, and yet foreign to me. From hence arise the most extraordinary self-contradictions. Without this influence from without, we should not perceive the power of discrimination. Such a power is the result of outer influence.

•

I know myself as I will myself to be, and I will because I know myself, because I am absolute in my own self. But I perceive on observation that I also have a will which works automatically, that I can both know and do without willing.

•

The spontaneous verdict is that man has a power beyond his individuality, but that he is denied the use of it. At every moment man is reminded that he is a supernatural being. If he were not, he would be no citizen of the world, only a beast.

•

Reflection and self-inspection are very difficult under such circumstances, as the inner life is so complicated with material vicissitudes. The more familiar reflection becomes to us, the more animating, powerful, and satisfactory are the conclusions we attain to – faith is a genuine act of revelation to the spirit. It is neither hearing, nor seeing, nor feeling – it is a combination of all three; but above them all, a sensation of absolute certainty, a comprehension of the truest life. Thoughts develop into laws, wishes become fulfilment. The *factum* of the moment is an article of faith to the weak. It is remarkable how we are affected at the sight of some human beings, the hearing of certain words, the reading of various passages. Accidental occurrences, the seasons, and natural events all influence us. Certain moods are favourable to these influences. They are generally instantaneous; few linger, fewer still abide with us. There is much difference of susceptibility among people. Some have a greater power of receiving impressions, others have more of a reasoning faculty, others have more perception. In illness this becomes very perceptible; some patients have more feeling than reason, others more reason than feeling.

•

The more our senses are refined, the more readily will they discern individual character. To carry out one's own rise in a masterly way, the senses must be swayed by the rule of reason.

•

The art of carrying out one's own will – we must rule both body and soul. The body is the tool for the civilizing and improving of the world; we must train all the bodily powers. Individual development of the bodily powers produces development of the world.

•

How strange it is that the inner life of men is so little thought of, and treated in so spiritless a way. So-called psychology is a mere mask which has usurped the place in which godlike images should be enshrined. How little has philosophy done for the soul, or the soul for the outside world. Perception, imagination, judgment, are the poverty-stricken classifications of the inner universe of man. Not a word as to their marvellous blendings, forms, and transitions. It has never occurred to anyone to see what new powers might be latent within us.

•

Mathematics are aids to thought.

•

Their power of applicability is the test of their use.

•

Their basis is the union and sympathy of the universe.

•

Ciphers are like signs and words – appearances, revelations.

•

Pure mathematics treat of the universe of thought.

•

Wonders, as supernatural facts, are *amathematic* only there are no miracles in this sense. What are so called are made comprehensible by mathematics, for nothing is a miracle when examined by mathematics.

•

Genuine mathematics are the true element of the magician.

•

In music they appear as a revelation, a creating ideality, a heavenly visitant to men.

•

All enjoyment is music conjoined with mathematics. Mathematics are the highest form of life.

•

A man may be a great mathematician, and yet no arithmetician, and conversely, a man may be a great arithmetician, and unable to comprehend mathematics.

•

The genuine mathematician is an enthusiast *per se*. Without enthusiasm, no mathematics.

•

Mathematics are the life of the gods.

•

All spiritual messengers must have been mathematicians. Religion is pure mathematics.

•

Through theophany man attains to mathematics. Mathematicians are the only happy people. The mathematician knows everything. He is able to find out what he does not know.

•

Where science enters, action ceases. Calm reflection, heavenly quietism, is the atmosphere of science.

•

The true mathematician is at home in the East. In Europe he is warped by technicality.

- None really comprehend mathematics who do not undertake the study with reverence and devotion as a revelation from God.

- Every line is the axis of a world.

- A formula is a mathematical receipt.

- Ciphers are dogmas.

- Arithmetic is their pharmacy.

- Higher mathematics contain at last mere methods of abbreviation.

- All crooked lines take their rise from one another, as life springs from life.

- Mathematics are capable of endless perfection, as a convincing proof of the sympathy and ideality of nature and intelligence.

- It is possible that a marvellous structure of mystic figures underlies all nature and even history. Has not everything which exists a significant symmetry and strange cohesion? Cannot God reveal Himself in mathematics as well as in other sciences?

- Wonders alternate with natural phenomena. They mutually limit each other, and together form an harmonious whole. There is no wonder without natural phenomena, and *vice versa*.

- Nature is ideal. The true ideal is possible, practical, and necessary.

- Physics are nothing else than the education of the imagination.

-

Nature is a fossilized city of enchantment. Our latest experimental philosophers theorize on the construction of the universe, but seem to make no real definite progress. One must either be satisfied with mystery, or else work steadily with mind and brain to elucidate difficulties.

•

Has increase of cultivation produced changes in nature? Was nature always obedient to laws, and will she ever remain so?

•

One may say that the organization of nature is superior to that of man. Or one may assert that nature is far below him, and he is the superior being.

•

Nature seems part of a greater whole. Her intelligence, and fancy, and will seem to bear the same relation to ours as our bodies do to her body.

•

The world may be defined as a tree, of which we are the blossoms.

•

Nature employs all her members, although each has its own objects and is independent of the rest. In the human body the reverse takes place.

•

The world is the result of the most profound knowledge. Our own varied powers enable us to perceive this.

•

All bodies which possess a special attribute are limited as to the use of this quality. Qualities are subjective – a feminine principle. Energy is the manlike principle – the objective. All attraction arises from energy. Everything which attracts us agitates us.

•

Impulse and space resemble each other. Every body is a completed impulse.

•

Body is a space filled by individuality.

•

Soul a time filled by individuality.

•

Space is a precipitate of time – a necessary result of time.

•

The nature and individuality of each fossil is controlled by the nature and individuality of its planet, which again is limited by its system, and its relation to other systems, and so on. In the same way, man is limited by the conditions of human life in this planet and its system. We are limited beings, but shall not always be so.

•

Like produces like. The power of production arises from organic elasticity.

•

Feeling is organized action; sensation the comprehension of assimilated feelings.

•

Life is like light, capable of increase and diminution. Can it, like light, break into colour? The process of nutrition is not the cause, but the consequence of life.

•

Light is the symbol and agent of purity. Where light can neither separate nor unite it passes through. What can neither be bound nor severed is pure and simple. Transparent bodies seem to be in a higher stage, and to have a kind of consciousness.

•

The specific gravity of the earth is almost the same as that of the diamond. Possibly the core of the world is a diamond.

•

Nature possesses wit, humour, fancy, and so forth. We find Nature's caricatures among plants and animals. Nature is full of humour in animal life. Stones and plants bear the stamp of fancy. In human life, thrifty Nature adorns herself both with fancy and wit.

•

Flowers are cosmopolitans, and enduring. Animals strive to monopolize power.

•

Animals are irrational; their bodies bear that stamp. Man's body bears the impress of reason. Man's substance is polarized by nature. The world of man is as varied as his powers. The animal world is much lower and poorer.

•

The thought-organs are world-producing.

•

The heavenly bodies form a fourth kingdom.

•

Heaven is the soul of the star system; the stars form its body.

•

All agreeable feeling is fiction. All pleasant thoughts arouse the soul to sympathetic action.

•

He who confines his thoughts to the organism of the body, and pays no attention to its mysterious connection with the soul, can make but little progress.

•

Life is, perhaps, nothing else but the result of this union.

•

Humanity is the highest development in our planet, the star which unites it to a higher world – the eye uplifted to heaven.

•

Nothing is more free or more bound than the spirit. Only a spirit can be forced to do something.

•

What can be compelled is spirit, in so far as it can be controlled.

•

Life is a soul sickness. Action is suffering. Rest is the element of the soul.

•

Body, soul, and spirit are the elements of the world, as epics, lyrics, and drama are of poetry.

•

Freedom and eternity are united even as space and time. As the world and eternity fill space and time, so omnipotence and omniscience pervade – both those spheres. God is the sphere of virtue. The soul is a consonant body. The Hebrews called vowels the soul of the alphabet.

•

The body stands in the same relation to the world that the soul does to the spirit. Both courses commence with man and end in God. Both circumnavigators meet at corresponding points of their course. Both have to consider how to remain together in spite of their separation, and how to accomplish both journeys in company.

•

If God could make Himself man, He could also make Himself stone, plant, animal, or element. Perhaps there is a continuous salvation in nature.

•

A peculiar genius in penetrating the meaning of nature is essential to the experimentalist.

•

The real observer is an artist; he guesses at hidden meanings, and perceives among many appearances which are the truly important.

•

The study of nature requires genuine love and child-like simplicity, piercing intellect and calm reason. Real progress might be attained if a whole nation were seized with a passionate desire for investigation, and the citizens, united by this common bond, made researches in all directions, and built laboratories in every town.

•

Perhaps the soul of plants may be ethereal oil, and this may be the cause of the varieties in wine.

●

Light is indisputably an electric product.

●

Thought is certainly electricity; the earthly spirit and its spiritual atmosphere are acted on by a heavenly supernatural spirit.

●

Body and soul affect each other electrically.

●

The spirit galvanizes the soul, buried as it is in the senses. Its activity is electricity.

●

If our bodily life is a burning, our spirit life may be a combustion (or is it the inverse?). Death is an alteration of power.

●

The soul deoxidates. Hence sleep, thought, and emotion cause bodily weakness and trembling. It may be that thought oxidates, and emotion deoxidates.

●

Ritter's views upon the formation and disappearance of matter throw light upon death. Who knows where we appear when we disappear from hence? Have all worlds the same form of production? The influence of the sun makes it possible that we may be transplanted there.

●

Nature is opposed to permanent possession. She destroys all personal landmarks, according to fixed laws. All races have equal rights to the earth. The earlier races owe their primogeniture to no special favour. At fixed epochs the right of possession lapses. Rise and decline are subject to laws. If the body is a property which bestows on me the rights of world citizen, I need not look on its loss as a penalty. I only lose my place in the royal school, that I may join a nobler association, where my beloved fellow-students will follow me.

•

Sleep is a condition in which body and soul are blended, as it were chemically. The soul pervades the whole body. Man is neutralized. Waking is a polarized state. The soul is localized. Sleep nourishes the soul, and so does the body. In a waking state the body feeds on the soul.

•

If cold really strengthens the muscles, then wit, humour, and jests must invigorate the spiritual muscles. Hence a mixture of what is merry with what is serious – the interweaving of the solemn and the laughable – might have good results.

• Thought and force belong to opposite spheres. What increases one diminishes the other. What develops the one dwarfs the other. The human body consists of thought and force, and their organs, nerves and muscles.

•

Man is distinguished from plants and animals by his tendency to disease. Man is born to suffer. The more helpless he is, the more sensitive to morality and religion.

•

Love is a disease. Hence the marvellous meaning of Christianity.

•

The soul is the strongest of all poisons. It has a subtle, penetrating charm. Hence all mental agitations are highly dangerous to sick persons.

•

May not disease be curable by disease? Every special organ, liver, lungs, gall, kidneys, & c., maintains its own identity and carries out its own functions. Each is a living concretion.

•

Polypi, cancer, and gangrene are perfect beasts of prey, or animal-plants. They grow, they produce, they have a special organization.

•

There is but one temple in the world, the human body. Nothing is holier than this form. Bowing to men is a recognition of this revelation in the flesh. One touches heaven when one touches a human being.

•

Man is like the sun. His senses are like planets. Man expresses a symbolic philosophy in his works and actions, his commissions and omissions. He is the Messiah of nature.

•

The more intellectual and cultivated a man is, the more individuality is seen in his members – his eyes, his hands, his fingers, & c. Our lips bear a great resemblance to the will-o'-thewisps in Goethe's fairy tales. The eyes are the elder sisters of the lips, they open and shut a holier sanctuary than the mouth. The ears are serpents which suck in what the lips utter. Mouth and eyes are similar in form. The eyelids are lips, the eyeball the tongue and palate, the pupil, the throat. The nose is the forehead of the mouth, and the brow the nose of the eyes. Each eye has its chin in the cheek-bone.

# HYMNS TO THE NIGHT[1]

What living, feeling being loves not the gorgeous hues which proclaim the dawn of day? The ever-moving stars, as they whirl in boundless ether, hail the dawn – bright herald of the day; the glistening rocks hail its rays, the tender, growing plants raise their pure eyes rejoicing, and the wild animal joins in the happy chorus which welcomes another day.

More than all these rejoices the glorious Being, the Monarch of the Earth. His deep, thoughtful eyes survey His creation, His melodious voice summons nature to resume her magic works. He binds or looses a million ties, and stamps all earthly life with some impress of His power. His presence reveals the marvels of the Kingdom of Earth. But sacred Night, with her unspoken mysteries, draws me to her. The world is far, far away, buried in a deep and lonely grave. My heart is full of sadness. Let me dissolve in drops of dew, and join the beloved dust. Long past memories, youthful ambitions, childhood's dreams, a long life of brief joys and blighted hopes, pass before me – dusky forms, like evening mist. In another region merry day returns triumphant. Will it never return to us, its children, who await its coming in childlike trust? What stirs this weary heart, and banishes my sorrow? Dost thou feel pity for us, O holy Night?

What soothing influence pervades my being? What hand sheds costly opiate on my throbbing heart? The wings of fancy no

1 This is parts 1 to 5, about a third of *Hymns To the Night*.

longer droop, fresh energy arises within me. In joyful surprise I see a calm, grave face bend lovingly over me, the face of a tender mother, beaming with eternal youth. How poor and childish in comparison are the joys of day. How blessed and consoling the return of night. The active work of day is over, the boundless ocean of space, with its lustrous spheres, proclaims Night's eternal power and presence. The eyes of the Night are countless hosts of glittering orbs, a glory far exceeding that of Day. They see far beyond the most distant of those countless hosts; they need no light to perceive the unfathomable depth of that loving Spirit who fills boundless space with happiness. All hail! Queen of the Earth! thou herald of holier worlds, thou revealer of holy love! Much loved sun of the night, thou art her gift.

My whole being awakes. I am thine, and thou art mine. Night has aroused me to life and manhood. Consume my earthly frame, draw me into deeper and closer union, and may our bridal night endure for ever.

2

Must Day return again? Will earthly influences never cease? Unholy toil desecrates the heavenly calm of Night. When shall the mystic sacrifice of love burn for ever? Light has its own fixed limits, but Night has a boundless unfathomable dominion; the reign of Sleep has no end. Holy Sleep! shed thy blest balm on the hallowed Night of this earthly sphere. Only fools fail to understand Thee, and know of no other sleep than the shades which the actual night casts over us in kindly pity. They see Thee not in the purple blood of the grape, in the golden oil of the almond, in the dusky sap of the poppy. They guess not that it is Thou who hoverest around the tender maiden, making her heart the temple of Heaven; nor dream that it is Thou, heavenly messenger, who bearest the key which opens the dwellings of the Blessed.

3

Once, as I shed bitter tears, all my hope dissolved in pain, as I stood alone by the grave which hid from my sight, in its dark narrow space, the form of my life; lonely as none had ever been, pursued by unspeakable anguish, powerless even to express my grief. I looked around for help. Forward I could not go – nor backward, but clung with unutterable longing to a transient extinguished life. Lo! from the azure distance, down from the heights of my old happiness, came a chill breath of dusk, which severed at once the bonds of birth, the fetters of light. Earthly glory vanished, bearing with it the sorrows of my heart; my sadness had fallen from me into an unknown, unfathomable world. Spirit of Night, heavenly rest, overshadowed me. My enfranchised new-born soul soared over the gently rising scene. The lonely grave turned to a cloud of dust, and through the cloud I discerned the transfigured features of my beloved. Eternity shone in her eyes, I clasped her hand, my tears formed a brilliant indissoluble chain. Eons of ages fled into space like scattered clouds. On her neck I wept the rapturous tears of the new life – it was my first, my only dream; and ever since I feel this changeless, everlasting faith in the heaven of Night and its light – my beloved.

I know when the last day shall come – when Light no longer shall be scared by Night and Love: then slumber shall not cease, and existence shall become an endless dream. Heavenly weariness oppresses me – long and dreamy was my pilgrimage to the Holy Grave, crushing was the cross I bore. He who has drunk of the crystal wave, which wells forth from the gloomy grave, on which earth's billows break, he who has stood on earth's border-land, and perceived that new country, the dwelling of Night, returns not to the tumult of life, to the land where light reigns amid ceaseless unrest. He builds himself a refuge far from the tumult – a peaceful home, and awaits the welcome hour, when he, too, shall be drawn into the crystal wave. All that savours of earth floats on the surface, and is driven back by tempests, but what love has hallowed flows in hidden channels, to another region where it mingles – a fragrant essence – with those loved ones who have fallen asleep.

Ah! merry Light, thou still arousest the weary to their task, and strivest to inspire me, too, with cheerful life; but thou hast no charm to tempt me from my cherished memories. With joy I watch the busy hands, and look around to fulfil my own duty, I praise thy glorious works, admire the matchless blending of thy cunning designs, watch the varied workings of the busy hours, and seek to discover the symmetry and laws which rule the marvels of endless space and measureless ages. But my heart remains ever true to Night and her daughter, creative Love. Canst thou show me one ever-faithful heart? Has thy sun a friendly glance for me? Do thy stars hold out a welcoming hand?

Do they return the gentle pressure and the caressing word? Hast thou clothed them in colour and beauty?' What joys or pleasure can life offer to outweigh the chain of death. Does not all that inspires us bear the colours of Night? Night bears thee gently like a mother; to her thou owest all thy glory. Thou wouldest have sunk into endless space, had not Night upheld thee, and bound thee, till earth arose. Truly existed long ere thou wert: I and my sisters were sent to dwell in thy world, and hallow it with love, to make it an enduring memorial; to plant it with unfading flowers. Not yet have these blossoms opened, few are the traces which mark our way. But the end of time is at hand; then thou wilt rejoin us, and gently fade away, full of longing and fervent desire. All thy busy restlessness will end in heavenly freedom, a blessed home-coming. With bitter grief I acknowledge thy forsaking of our home, thine unconquered hatred to the old glorious heaven.

But in vain is Thy wrath and fury. The Cross stands firm for ever, the banner of our race.

The many scattered races of mankind lay bound for ages in the grasp of an iron fate. Light was hidden from their weary souls. The eternal world was the home and dwelling of the Gods. Its mysterious form had existed from eternity. Over the glowing mountains of the East abode the Sun, with its all-pervading heat and light. An aged Giant bore the Earth on his shoulders. The Titans, the first children of Mother Earth – who had waged impious war against the new glorious race of Gods and their kinsfolk, the merry race of men – lay fast bound under the mountains. The dark green depths of Ocean was the lap of a Goddess. A gay, luxurious race dwelt in the crystal grottoes. Beasts, trees, flowers, and animals had the gift of speech. Richer was the flavour of the grapes, for a God dwelt in the luxuriant vine; the golden sheaves took their birth from a loving motherly Goddess; and love was the sweet service rendered to the deities. Age followed age – a ceaseless spring, and the happy life of Earth's children was ever enlivened by celestial presences. All races honoured the flashing, many-hued flame, as the highest manifestation in life. Only one shadow obscured the common joy – the cruel spectre of Death. This mysterious decree – separation from all that was loved and lovely – weighed heavy on the hearts of all; even the Gods could find no remedy for this evil. Unable to overcome the menacing fate, man strove to cast a glamour of beauty over the ghastly phantom, and pictured him as a lovely youth extinguishing a torch, and sinking to rest. Still the cruel enigma remained unsolved, and spoke of the irresistible might of some unknown power. The old world waned; the flowers of the first Paradise faded away; and the race of men, casting off their early innocence, strayed into a wild, uncultivated desert. The Gods and their retinues vanished from Earth. Nature stood lonely and lifeless, bound in the iron chains of custom and laws. The bloom was brushed from life. Faith took flight from the dreary scene; and with her fled her heavenly companion Fancy, who could cast over all things her magic vesture. A cruel North wind swept over the barren waste, and the devastated wonder-home was blown into space. Heaven's blue ocean showed new dazzling spheres, and the Spirit of the World withdrew to higher regions to await the dawn of a renewed earth. Light ceased to be the abode and the symbol of the Gods; they covered themselves with the veil of Night. Night was the cradle of the coming age; in it the Gods took refuge, and sleep came upon them, until a new era should call them forth in new and more glorious forms. The new era arose at last amidst a nation scorned and despised, a people who had cast off their native innocence. In poverty was born the Son of the first Virgin Mother, mysterious offspring of heavenly origin. The wise sons of the East were first to acknowledge the commencement of the strange, new epoch, and humbly bent their way to worship the King in His lowly cradle – a mystic star guided their wandering steps. They did Him homage, offering Him the sweetness and brightness of the earth, the gold and the perfume, both miracles of nature. The Heavenly Heart unfolded slowly – a flower chalice of Almighty love, with eyes upturned to a Divine Father, while His head rested on the tender bosom of a loving earthly mother. With prophetic eye and godlike zeal, the blooming Child, despising the cruel days of earthly conflict before Him, looked far ahead to the future of His beloved face, the offshoots of a divine root. Soon He gathered around Him a loving band of childlike hearts. A strange, new life arose, like that of the flowers of the field; unceasing words of wisdom and utterances of deepest love fell from His lips, like sparks of divine fire. From the far shores of Hellas, and her sunny skies, the poet came to Palestine, and laid his heart at the feet of the Wonder-Child.

Oh! Thou art He who from unending years
Hast looked with pity on our earthly tomb;
Thou gav'st a sign of life in deepest night,

And Thou wilt bring our higher manhood home.
Thou hast upheld us here mid grief and tears.
Lead Thou our nobler longings up to Heaven;
In death alone eternal life is found.
For Thou art death, and Thou our life hast given.

Full of joy, his heart beating with new love and hope, the singer bent his way to Hindustan, pouring out under its cloudless sky such burning songs, that myriads of hearts turned to him, and the joyful news spread far and near. Soon after the poet left, the precious Life fell a sacrifice to fallen man: He died young, torn away from the much-loved earth, His weeping mother, and His faint-hearted friends. The moment of anguish, the birth of the new world was at hand. He fought with the old dreaded form of death; struggled hard to shake off the clutch of the old world; His sweet lips drained the bitter chalice of unspeakable anguish. Once more He cast a loving glance at His mother, then came the delivering hand of Mighty Love, and He fell asleep. For many days a thick mist lay on the raging waters and the quaking earth: countless were the tears shed by those who loved Him: the secret of the grave was made clear, and heavenly spirits rolled away the heavy stone from the tomb. Angels watched by the slumbering Form: rising in new godlike glory, He soared to the heights of the newly-made world, buried the old earthly shape in the depths of a cavern, and laid His mighty hand on it, so that no power might ever move it.

The loving ones still wept by His grave, but they wept tears of emotion and gratitude. Again they see Thee and rejoice at Thy resurrection: they see Thee weeping on Thy mother's sacred bosom: they walk once more as friends, listening to words like leaves fluttering from the Tree of Life: they behold Thee hasten with untold longing to the Father's arms, bearing aloft the new manhood and the victorious chalice. The mother soon hastened to join Thy triumph: she was the first to enter the New Home. Long years have passed since *then* and Thy new creation soars to higher powers: thousands and thousands drawn by Thee from bitter grief and pain now roam with Thee and the heavenly Virgin in the Kingdom of Love, serve in the Temple of Divine Death, and are Thine eternally.

# Bibliography

BY NOVALIS

Recommended books are marked with an asterisk.

*Novalis Schriften. Die Werke Friedrichs von Hardenberg*, ed. Richard Samuel, Hans-Joachim Mähl & Gerhard Schulz, Kohlhammer, Stuttgart, 1960-88 *
*Pollen and Fragments: Selected Poetry and Prose*, tr. Arthur Versluis, Phanes Press, Grand Rapids, 1989 *
*Hymns to the Night and Other Selected Writings*, tr. Charles E. Passage, Bobbs-Merrill Company, Indianapolis, 1960
*Hymns to the Night*, Treacle Press, New York, NY, 1978 *
*Novalis: Fichte Studies*, ed. J. Kneller, Cambridge University Press, Cambridge, 2003
*Notes For a Romantic Encyclopedia*, tr. D. Wood, State University of New York Press, New York, 2007


ON NOVALIS

Henri Clemens Birven. *Novalis, Magus der Romantik*, Schwab, Büdingen, 1959
B. Donehower, ed. *The Birth of Novalis*, State University of New York Press, New York, 2007
Sara Frierichsmeyer. *The Androgyne in Early German Romanticism: Friedrich Schlegel, Novalis and the Metaphysics of Love*, Bern, New York, 1983
Curt Grutzmacher. *Novalis und Philippe Otto Runge*, Eidos, Munich 1964
Bruce Haywood. *The Veil of Imagery: A Study of the Poetic Works of Friedrich von Hardenburg*, Harvard University Press, Cambridge,

Mass., 1959

Frederick Heibel. *Novalis: German Poet, European Thinker, Christian Mystic*, AMS, New York, 1969

L. Johns. *The Art of Recollection in Jena Romanticism*, Niemeyer, Tübingen, 2002

Alice Kuzniar. *Delayed Endings: Nonclosure in Novalis and Hölderlin*, University of Georgia Press, Athens, 1987

Géza von Molnar. *Novalis's Fichte Studies*, Mouton, The Hague 1970

—. *Romantic Vision, Ethical Context: Novalis and Artistic Autonomy*, University of Minnesota Press, Minneapolis 1987

Bruno Müller. *Novalis – der dichter als Mittler*, Lang, Bern, 1984

John Neubauer. *Bifocal Vision: Novalis's Philosophy of Nature and Disease*, Chapel Hill 1972

—. *Novalis*, 1980

I. Nikolova. *Complementary Modes of Representation in Keats, Novalis and Shelley*, Peter Lang, New York, 2001

Nicholas Saul. *History and Poetry in Novalis and in the Tradition of the German Enlightenment*, Institute of Germanic Studies, 1984


## OTHERS


Gwendolyn Bays. *The Orphic Vision: Seer Poets from Novalis to Rimbaud*, University of Nebraska Press, Lincoln, 1964 *

Ernst Behler. *German Romantic Literary Theory*, Cambridge University Press, 1993 *

Ernst Benz. *The Mystical Sources of German Romantic Philosophy*, tr. B. Reynolds & E. Paul, Pickwick, Allison Park, 1983

G. Birrell. *The Boundless Presence: Space and Time In the Literary Fairy Tales of Novalis and Tieck*, 1979

Richard Brinkmann, ed. *Romantik in Deutschland*, Metzler, Stuttgart, 1978

Manfred Brown. *The Shape of German Romanticism*, Cornell University Press, Ithaca, 1979

K. Calhoun. *Fatherland: Novalis, Freud and the Discipline of Romance*, 1992

Manfred Dick. *Die Entwicklung des Gedankens der Poesie in den Fragmenten des Novalis*, Bouvier, Bonn, 1967, 223-77

Hans Eichner. *Friedrich Schlegel*, Twayne, New York, 1970

R.W. Ewton. *The Literary Theory of A.W. Schlegel*, Mouthon, The Hague, 1971

Richard Faber. *Novalis: die Phantasie an die Macht*, Metzler, Stuttgart 1970

Walter Feilchenfeld. *Der Einfluss Jacob Böhmes auf Novalis*, Eberia, Berlin, 1922

Theodor Haering. *Novalis als Philosoph*, Kohlhammer, Stuttgart, 1954

Michael Hamburger. *Reason and Energy: Studies in German Literature*, Weidenfeld & Nicolson, 1970 *

Heinrich Heine. *The Complete Poems of Heinrich Heine*, tr. Hal Draper, Suhrkamp/ Insel, Boston, 1982

—. *The North Sea*, tr. Vernon Watkins, Faber, 1955

Friedrich Hölderlin. *Poems and Fragments*, tr. Michael Hamburger, Routledge & Kegan Paul, 1966

Glyn Tegai Hughes. *Romantic German Literature*, Edward Arnold, 1979 *

Philippe Lacoue-Labarthe & Jean-Luc Nancy, eds. *The Literary Absolute: The Theory of Literature in German Romanticism*, State University of New York Press, Albany, 1988

D. Mahoney. *The Critical Fortunes of a Romantic Novel*, 1994

J. Neubauer. *Novalis*, 1980

W. O'Brien. *Novalis*, 1995

Ritchie Robertson. *Heine*, Peter Halban, 1988

Helmut Schanze. *Romantik und Aufklärung, Unterschungen zu Friedrich Schlegel und Novalis*, Carl, Nürnberg, 1966

—. ed. *Friedrich Schlegel und die Kunstheorie Seiner Zeit*, Wissenschaftliche Buchgesellschaft, Darmstadt, 1985

Elizabeth Sewell. *The Orphic Voice: Poetry and Natural History*, Routledge, 1961*

Karl Heinz Volkmann-Schluck. "Novalis' magischer Idealismus", *Die deutsche Romantik*, ed. Hans Steffen, 1967, 45-53

WEBSITES

| | |
|---|---|
| Aquarium | novalis.autorenverzeichnis.de |
| Novalis Gesellschaft | novalis-gesellschaft.de |
| International Novalis Society | ula.org/s/or/en |

# CRESCENT MOON PUBLISHING

web: www.crmoon.com e-mail: cresmopub@yahoo.co.uk

## ARTS, PAINTING, SCULPTURE

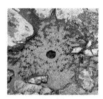

The Art of Andy Goldsworthy
Andy Goldsworthy: Touching Nature
Andy Goldsworthy in Close-Up
Andy Goldsworthy: Pocket Guide
Andy Goldsworthy In America
Land Art: A Complete Guide
The Art of Richard Long
Richard Long: Pocket Guide
Land Art In the UK
Land Art in Close-Up
Land Art In the U.S.A.
Land Art: Pocket Guide
Installation Art in Close-Up
Minimal Art and Artists In the 1960s and After
Colourfield Painting
Land Art DVD, TV documentary
Andy Goldsworthy DVD, TV documentary
The Erotic Object: Sexuality in Sculpture From Prehistory to the Present Day
Sex in Art: Pornography and Pleasure in Painting and Sculpture
Postwar Art
Sacred Gardens: The Garden in Myth, Religion and Art
Glorification: Religious Abstraction in Renaissance and 20th Century Art
Early Netherlandish Painting
Leonardo da Vinci
Piero della Francesca
Giovanni Bellini
Fra Angelico: Art and Religion in the Renaissance
Mark Rothko: The Art of Transcendence
Frank Stella: American Abstract Artist
Jasper Johns
Brice Marden
Alison Wilding: The Embrace of Sculpture
Vincent van Gogh: Visionary Landscapes
Eric Gill: Nuptials of God
Constantin Brancusi: Sculpting the Essence of Things
Max Beckmann
Caravaggio
Gustave Moreau
Egon Schiele: Sex and Death In Purple Stockings
Delizioso Fotografico Fervore: Works In Process 1
Sacro Cuore: Works In Process 2
The Light Eternal: J.M.W. Turner
The Madonna Glorified: Karen Arthurs

# LITERATURE

J.R.R. Tolkien: The Books, The Films, The Whole Cultural Phenomenon
J.R.R. Tolkien: Pocket Guide
Tolkien's Heroic Quest
The *Earthsea* Books of Ursula Le Guin
Beauties, Beasts and Enchantment: Classic French Fairy Tales
German Popular Stories by the Brothers Grimm
Philip Pullman and *His Dark Materials*
Sexing Hardy: Thomas Hardy and Feminism
Thomas Hardy's *Tess of the d'Urbervilles*
Thomas Hardy's *Jude the Obscure*
Thomas Hardy: The Tragic Novels
Love and Tragedy: Thomas Hardy
The Poetry of Landscape in Hardy
Wessex Revisited: Thomas Hardy and John Cowper Powys
Wolfgang Iser: Essays and Interviews
Petrarch, Dante and the Troubadours
Maurice Sendak and the Art of Children's Book Illustration
Andrea Dworkin
Cixous, Irigaray, Kristeva: The *Jouissance* of French Feminism
Julia Kristeva: Art, Love, Melancholy, Philosophy, Semiotics and Psychoanalysis
Hélene Cixous I Love You: The *Jouissance* of Writing
Luce Irigaray: Lips, Kissing, and the Politics of Sexual Difference
Peter Redgrove: Here Comes the Flood
Peter Redgrove: Sex-Magic-Poetry-Cornwall
Lawrence Durrell: Between Love and Death, East and West
Love, Culture & Poetry: Lawrence Durrell
Cavafy: Anatomy of a Soul
German Romantic Poetry: Goethe, Novalis, Heine, Hölderlin
Feminism and Shakespeare
Shakespeare: Love, Poetry & Magic
The Passion of D.H. Lawrence
D.H. Lawrence: Symbolic Landscapes
D.H. Lawrence: Infinite Sensual Violence
Rimbaud: Arthur Rimbaud and the Magic of Poetry
The Ecstasies of John Cowper Powys
Sensualism and Mythology: The Wessex Novels of John Cowper Powys
Amorous Life: John Cowper Powys and the Manifestation of Affectivity  (H.W. Fawkner)
Postmodern Powys: New Essays on John Cowper Powys (Joe Boulter)
Rethinking Powys: Critical Essays on John Cowper Powys
Paul Bowles & Bernardo Bertolucci
Rainer Maria Rilke
Joseph Conrad: *Heart of Darkness*
In the Dim Void: Samuel Beckett
Samuel Beckett Goes into the Silence
André Gide: Fiction and Fervour
Jackie Collins and the Blockbuster Novel
Blinded By Her Light: The Love-Poetry of Robert Graves
The Passion of Colours: Travels In Mediterranean Lands
Poetic Forms

# POETRY

Ursula Le Guin: Walking In Cornwall
Peter Redgrove: Here Comes The Flood
Peter Redgrove: Sex-Magic-Poetry-Cornwall
Dante: Selections From the Vita Nuova
Petrarch, Dante and the Troubadours
William Shakespeare: Sonnets
William Shakespeare: Complete Poems
Blinded By Her Light: The Love-Poetry of Robert Graves
Emily Dickinson: Selected Poems
Emily Brontë: Poems
Thomas Hardy: Selected Poems
Percy Bysshe Shelley: Poems
John Keats: Selected Poems
Joh n Keats: Poems of 1820
D.H. Lawrence: Selected Poems
Edmund Spenser: Poems
Edmund Spenser: Amoretti
John Donne: Poems
Henry Vaughan: Poems
Sir Thomas Wyatt: Poems
Robert Herrick: Selected Poems
Rilke: Space, Essence and Angels in the Poetry of Rainer Maria Rilke
Rainer Maria Rilke: Selected Poems
Friedrich Hölderlin: Selected Poems
Arseny Tarkovsky: Selected Poems
Arthur Rimbaud: Selected Poems
Arthur Rimbaud: A Season in Hell
Arthur Rimbaud and the Magic of Poetry
Novalis: Hymns To the Night
German Romantic Poetry
Paul Verlaine: Selected Poems
Elizaethan Sonnet Cycles
D.J. Enright: By-Blows
Jeremy Reed: Brigitte's Blue Heart
Jeremy Reed: Claudia Schiffer's Red Shoes
Gorgeous Little Orpheus
Radiance: New Poems
Crescent Moon Book of Nature Poetry
Crescent Moon Book of Love Poetry
Crescent Moon Book of Mystical Poetry
Crescent Moon Book of Elizabethan Love Poetry
Crescent Moon Book of Metaphysical Poetry
Crescent Moon Book of Romantic Poetry
Pagan America: New American Poetry

# MEDIA, CINEMA, FEMINISM and CULTURAL STUDIES

J.R.R. Tolkien: The Books, The Films, The Whole Cultural Phenomenon
J.R.R. Tolkien: Pocket Guide
The *Lord of the Rings* Movies: Pocket Guide
The Cinema of Hayao Miyazaki
Hayao Miyazaki: *Princess Mononoke*: Pocket Movie Guide
Hayao Miyazaki: *Spirited Away*: Pocket Movie Guide
Tim Burton : Hallowe'en For Hollywood
Ken Russell
Ken Russell: *Tommy*: Pocket Movie Guide
The Ghost Dance: The Origins of Religion
The Peyote Cult
Cixous, Irigaray, Kristeva: The *Jouissance* of French Feminism
Julia Kristeva: Art, Love, Melancholy, Philosophy, Semiotics and Psychoanalysis
Luce Irigaray: Lips, Kissing, and the Politics of Sexual Difference
Hélene Cixous I Love You: The *Jouissance* of Writing
Andrea Dworkin
'Cosmo Woman': The World of Women's Magazines
Women in Pop Music
HomeGround: The Kate Bush Anthology
Discovering the Goddess (Geoffrey Ashe)
The Poetry of Cinema
The Sacred Cinema of Andrei Tarkovsky
Andrei Tarkovsky: Pocket Guide
Andrei Tarkovsky: *Mirror*: Pocket Movie Guide
Andrei Tarkovsky: *The Sacrifice*: Pocket Movie Guide
Walerian Borowczyk: Cinema of Erotic Dreams
Jean-Luc Godard: The Passion of Cinema
Jean-Luc Godard: *Hail Mary*: Pocket Movie Guide
Jean-Luc Godard: *Contempt*: Pocket Movie Guide
Jean-Luc Godard: *Pierrot le Fou*: Pocket Movie Guide
John Hughes and Eighties Cinema
*Ferris Bueller's Day Off*: Pocket Movie Guide
Jean-Luc Godard: Pocket Guide
The Cinema of Richard Linklater
Liv Tyler: Star In Ascendance
*Blade Runner* and the Films of Philip K. Dick
Paul Bowles and Bernardo Bertolucci
Media Hell: Radio, TV and the Press
An Open Letter to the BBC
Detonation Britain: Nuclear War in the UK
Feminism and Shakespeare
Wild Zones: Pornography, Art and Feminism
Sex in Art: Pornography and Pleasure in Painting and Sculpture
Sexing Hardy: Thomas Hardy and Feminism

*The Light Eternal* is a model monograph, an exemplary job. The subject matter of the book is beautifully organised and dead on beam. (Lawrence Durrell)

It is amazing for me to see my work treated with such passion and respect. (Andrea Dworkin)

CRESCENT MOON PUBLISHING
P.O. Box 1312, Maidstone, Kent, ME14 5XU, Great Britain. www.crmoon.com

cresmopub@yahoo.co.uk   www.crescentmoon.org.uk